# The Black Dahlia Murder and Its Unanswered Questions

*An Exhaustive New Look at the Evidence, Suspects, and Theories Behind One of the Most Infamous Cold Cases*

**Pamela O. Parker**

# Table of contents

# Preface

## *Introduction to the Black Dahlia Case*

The Black Dahlia murder, one of the most notorious and enduring unsolved crimes in American history, continues to haunt the collective imagination of the public, criminologists, and conspiracy theorists alike. The tragic death of Elizabeth Short in January 1947, and the mystery surrounding her brutal murder, captivated the United States and became a symbol of the macabre in a city already famous for its darker undercurrents— the sprawling, glamorous, and often dangerous Hollywood of the mid-20th century.

Elizabeth Short, a 22-year-old woman from Medford, Massachusetts, had dreams of becoming an actress. She had come to Los Angeles in the late 1940s with hopes of making it in the film industry, but she found herself living a transient, somewhat troubled life. Short, who was often described as strikingly beautiful and enigmatic, had a complex and at times troubled personal history. Despite her aspirations, she was working odd jobs and often found herself at the mercy of difficult relationships. In the end, she would become famous for reasons entirely out of her control—her violent and highly publicized murder.

On January 15, 1947, Elizabeth's body was discovered in a vacant lot on the west side of Los Angeles. The crime scene was horrific. Her body had been bisected at the waist, drained of blood, and posed in an unsettling manner. The violence of the crime and the bizarre manner in which the body was arranged shocked the nation. Headlines across the country screamed about the brutality of the murder and the mystery surrounding the identity of the killer. The investigation that followed would become one of the most high-profile in American law enforcement history, drawing attention not only for its gruesome nature but also for its baffling lack of resolution.

Despite an intense investigation, hundreds of leads, and widespread media coverage, no one has ever been definitively convicted for Elizabeth Short's murder. Over the years, several suspects have been named, but the case remains cold to this day. The Black Dahlia case has inspired countless books, films, documentaries, and conspiracy theories, each attempting to uncover the truth behind Elizabeth Short's tragic death. This book aims to explore the details of this infamous crime, examine the investigations and theories surrounding it, and understand why it has continued to captivate the public's interest for so many decades.

**Purpose of the Book**

The purpose of this book is to provide a comprehensive examination of the Black Dahlia murder, not only from the perspective of the investigation but also through a broader lens that considers its impact on American culture and society. While numerous books have been written about Elizabeth Short's murder and its many theories, this book seeks to offer a fresh perspective—one that is both deeply respectful to the life of the victim and rigorously analytical about the various aspects of the case.

The book will explore several key dimensions:

1. **The Life of Elizabeth Short**: To understand her murder, we must first understand who Elizabeth Short was. This book delves into her early life in Massachusetts, her move to California, her personal relationships, and the events leading up to her tragic death. By doing so, we aim to provide a more humanized portrait of Short, a woman who has been reduced to a tragic symbol in the public eye.

2. **The Crime Scene and Investigation**: The circumstances surrounding the discovery of Elizabeth Short's body are horrifying. The book will analyze the crime scene, the forensic evidence (or lack thereof), and the initial investigations. It will also cover the various police leads, suspects, and theories that arose in the aftermath of the murder, providing insight into the challenges investigators faced and the failures that led to the case remaining unsolved.

3. **The Media Sensationalism**: In 1947, Los Angeles was a media epicenter, and the Black

Dahlia case became a cultural phenomenon. The press sensationalized Elizabeth Short's life and death, often distorting the truth and perpetuating myths about her. This book will explore how the media played a crucial role in shaping the narrative around the Black Dahlia, transforming Elizabeth Short into a symbol of both the dark side of Hollywood and the vulnerability of young women in post-war America.

4. **Theories and Suspects**: Over the years, numerous suspects have been identified in the Black Dahlia case. Some have been dismissed, while others have become the subject of intense speculation. This book will take an in-depth look at these suspects, examining the evidence against them, the reasons they became prominent in the investigation, and how their involvement (or lack thereof) has shaped the ongoing mystery.

5. **The Cultural Impact**: The Black Dahlia case has left an indelible mark on popular culture, inspiring films, books, music, and art. The book will discuss the enduring legacy of the Black Dahlia, how it has influenced crime fiction and Hollywood storytelling, and why it continues to capture the public's fascination. The case is not just a historical incident but a symbol of the tensions between fame, violence, and the pursuit of truth.

6.  **Unresolved Questions**: Perhaps most compelling of all is the fact that Elizabeth Short's murder remains unsolved to this day. The book will examine the reasons behind this, discussing the police's mistakes, missteps, and missed opportunities, as well as the broader implications of an unsolved murder in an age of growing public interest in true crime.

By the end of this book, readers will have gained a deeper understanding of not just the facts surrounding the Black Dahlia case but also the complexities of its ongoing impact. The book does not promise to provide the definitive answer to who killed Elizabeth Short, but rather to examine the various elements of the case and its legacy from a multifaceted perspective.

Through rigorous research, careful analysis, and thoughtful examination, this book seeks to illuminate the story of the Black Dahlia—both the woman who became the tragic victim of a brutal crime and the case that has remained an enduring mystery for over seventy years. It is a story of loss, fear, and the unanswered questions that continue to haunt us, reminding us of the shadowy corners of fame, ambition, and violence that define modern life.

## Why This Case Still Matters

The Black Dahlia case endures not simply because of the shocking nature of the crime but because it embodies a larger narrative about the dark side of the American

Dream. Elizabeth Short, a young woman with big dreams of stardom, met with the brutal violence that was a hidden part of the glamour and illusion of Hollywood. Her death revealed the murky underside of the city, where fame could become as dangerous as it was alluring. For the police, it was a high-profile case that garnered national attention. For the media, it was an opportunity to sell sensationalized stories and narratives. And for the public, it became a symbol of the dangers of fame and the complexities of criminal justice.

The question of "who killed Elizabeth Short?" will likely remain unanswered for the foreseeable future. Yet the search for the truth, combined with the emotional weight of the crime, is what continues to draw people to the case. Elizabeth Short's life and death have become a symbol of the fear and fascination that crime, mystery, and the desire for truth provoke in us all.

As we move forward, this book aims to keep the memory of Elizabeth Short alive—not just as a victim but as a woman whose life was marked by both ambition and tragedy. The Black Dahlia case is more than a mystery; it is a reflection of the broader human experience, shaped by our desires, our fears, and our need for justice.

# Part I: The Life of Elizabeth Short

# Chapter 1

## Early Life and Background

Elizabeth Short was born on July 29, 1924, in Boston, Massachusetts, to Cleo Short and Phoebe Mae (née Garrison) Short. Her early years, unlike the grim fate that would later define her, were filled with the promise of a typical American childhood, albeit one marked by the kind of turbulence and hardship that often shapes a person's path in life.

### *Family, Childhood, and Upbringing*

Elizabeth, known as "Betty" to her family, was the third of five children. Her family had its share of difficulties, beginning with the tragic early death of her father. Cleo Short, a man who had initially supported his family as a car salesman and later worked at various odd jobs, mysteriously disappeared in 1926 when Elizabeth was only two years old. He was later presumed dead, although there is speculation and conflicting reports about his fate. Some believe he may have taken his own life by drowning in the Mystic River in Massachusetts, while others suggest that he simply abandoned his family.

In the absence of a father figure, Elizabeth's mother, Phoebe, was left to raise five children on her own. Phoebe struggled financially, but she did her best to provide a stable home life for her children. However, the absence of a male authority figure and the financial burden placed significant stress on the family dynamics. In Elizabeth's case, this period of instability would shape her future in profound ways.

As a child, Elizabeth was described as intelligent and ambitious, with an adventurous spirit. She was known to be quiet and reserved, but also very charming when she warmed to someone. Her childhood, though not easy, was filled with the typical joys of growing up in the 1920s and 1930s. Like many young girls of the time, she dreamed of becoming a movie star. Elizabeth's beauty, which would later play a significant role in her tragic story, was evident even at a young age. With her striking dark features, porcelain skin, and penetrating eyes, she had the kind of appearance that would catch the eye of anyone who crossed her path.

However, the Short family's precarious economic situation often meant that Elizabeth and her siblings were moving from place to place, trying to make ends meet. The family lived in various locations throughout Massachusetts and New England, from Medford to Weymouth. Elizabeth's mother, Phoebe, took on numerous jobs to support the family, but the financial strain was relentless. By all accounts, Elizabeth was a sensitive child, often caught between her mother's strictness and the absence of a stable father figure.

While Phoebe worked tirelessly to hold the family together, Elizabeth's yearning for independence and adventure grew. She was often described as a girl with an old soul, someone who thought deeply about life's struggles even from a young age. Elizabeth would later recall how she longed to escape from the confines of her small-town upbringing, dreaming of a glamorous life far away from the pressures and limitations of her surroundings. She wanted to make something of herself, to be recognized for her beauty and talents, and most of all, to be loved and adored—both by those close to her and the public.

## *Life Before Los Angeles*

At the age of 18, Elizabeth decided to leave Massachusetts and move to California, where she believed her dreams of becoming an actress could come true. In 1942, she moved to Florida to live with a family friend before heading out to California. Her first stop was Miami, where she worked briefly as a waitress. However, her aspirations were too big for this small stage. Elizabeth's beauty and ambitions would lead her westward, where she made her way to Los Angeles in the spring of 1943.

Upon arriving in Los Angeles, Elizabeth found herself in a city teeming with young women hoping to break into the Hollywood scene. It was a time when the city was dominated by the glamour of Tinseltown and the promise of fame lured many to the West Coast. Though Elizabeth was no different from the thousands of other aspiring actresses who flooded the city each year, her path would prove to be more tragic and complicated than most.

When Elizabeth first arrived in California, she lived with a series of relatives and friends in various parts of the city, and she found work as a waitress and occasional model. Her experiences were similar to many other women seeking fame, as she tried to make a name for herself in an industry that could be both alluring and dangerous. But despite her beauty and undeniable charm, Elizabeth never managed to land a major role or become the star she longed to be.

Throughout this period, Elizabeth became known for her enigmatic personality. She was strikingly beautiful, but her life was filled with instability and uncertainty. She was often described as a young woman who lived with one foot in the world of glamour and the other in a much darker reality. The contrast between her external persona and the inner turmoil she faced made her all the more fascinating to those who knew her. She developed a reputation for being friendly but distant, alluring yet elusive, and always striving for something more than what life was offering her.

While in Los Angeles, Elizabeth was also known for her interactions with men. Some accounts indicate that she had a series of brief relationships with men who were either drawn to her beauty or intrigued by her mysterious aura. Though none of these relationships led to anything permanent, they seemed to serve as a form of companionship during her lonely and often difficult years in California.

By 1946, Elizabeth had found herself in a precarious position—working odd jobs, living in a succession of temporary accommodations, and grappling with her own desires for success. Though she remained optimistic, she was also acutely aware that the Hollywood dream might not be within her reach. She was often described as a woman who was both hopeful and resigned at the same time, someone who constantly strived for more but was frequently confronted by the harsh realities of her situation.

## Dreams and Struggles

Despite her struggles, Elizabeth held onto her dream of becoming an actress, but the reality of Hollywood's cutthroat industry was far from the image she had imagined. The pressures of trying to make it in an industry known for its exploitation of young women were immense, and Elizabeth soon found herself caught up in the darker side of Los Angeles.

Her beauty, while captivating, became both an asset and a burden. Elizabeth was known for her striking appearance, with her dark hair, fair skin, and intense gaze. Yet, in a city where beauty was often commodified, her looks seemed to define her more than her personality or talents. As the years went by, she found herself moving from one temporary living arrangement to the next, unable to secure any lasting stability or a foothold in the entertainment world. The dream of becoming an actress remained elusive, and she soon became disillusioned with the promises of fame that had first drawn her to Los Angeles.

At the same time, Elizabeth's personal life began to unravel. She experienced a string of short-term relationships, but none of them seemed to provide the emotional fulfillment or stability she craved. In a 1946 letter to a friend, Elizabeth wrote about her feelings of loneliness and frustration, expressing her desire to escape the pressures of Los Angeles and find a sense of peace.

Despite the obstacles she faced, Elizabeth remained hopeful. In her letters and conversations with those closest to her, she often spoke of her belief that one day she would find the happiness and success she longed for. But tragically, her story would take a much darker turn in the months following these letters.

Though her time in Los Angeles was marked by hardship, Elizabeth's presence in the city was never entirely unnoticed. She was often seen in various parts of town, particularly around Hollywood Boulevard and the Sunset Strip, where she would walk among the crowds of dreamers, hopefuls, and tourists. To those who knew her, Elizabeth Short was a beautiful young woman with a quiet but magnetic presence. However, behind that allure was a young woman struggling with her own sense of identity, fighting to make sense of a world that offered her few answers.

As she moved deeper into the city's underbelly, Elizabeth's life was becoming increasingly disconnected from the glamorous world of Hollywood she had envisioned. Her final months, leading up to her tragic death, were marked by a series of strange and unexplained events that would only add to the mystery surrounding her. The shadow of the Black Dahlia would soon begin to take shape, and the glamorous dream of Hollywood would fade forever.

# Chapter 2

# Arrival in Hollywood

Elizabeth Short's journey to California was the beginning of a series of dramatic twists and turns that would ultimately culminate in one of the most infamous and tragic events in the history of Los Angeles. But before she arrived on the West Coast, Elizabeth had been living a life of hardship and instability...

## *Moving to California*

In 1943, Elizabeth Short, at the age of 19, left her home in Medford, Massachusetts, and set her sights on a life in California. She arrived in Los Angeles, a city that, for many young women across the country, symbolized hope, possibility, and the chance to reinvent oneself. Hollywood, the heart of the American film industry, was an alluring destination for those who dreamed of fame, glamour, and the bright lights of the silver screen. However, Elizabeth had no immediate connections or significant financial resources. Her journey was one of perseverance and the hope of a better life.

Her decision to leave Massachusetts was partly driven by her difficult family situation. Elizabeth's father, Cleo Short, had disappeared when she was a child, leaving her mother to raise her and her two sisters on her own. Elizabeth's mother had a volatile relationship with Cleo, and there were periods of financial struggle throughout Elizabeth's childhood. This environment likely fueled her desire for independence, something she believed she could find in California.

When Elizabeth arrived in California, she initially lived with friends in Santa Barbara and briefly worked in a number of unglamorous jobs, including at a local restaurant. It wasn't long before she made her way to Los Angeles, where she would begin her pursuit of fame. However, it's important to note that Elizabeth did not immediately arrive in Hollywood as an aspiring actress or starlet; her original goal was simply to find her place in a city that promised opportunities, even if they were difficult to come by.

## The Pursuit of Fame

Though Elizabeth's dreams were not immediately realized, she soon made connections with people who might have had the potential to propel her into the spotlight. As she began making her way through Los Angeles' social circles, she became known as a young, attractive woman with striking features and a mysterious demeanor. It was these qualities, paired with her striking physical appearance, that made her memorable to many.

Elizabeth's physical traits—dark brown hair, piercing blue eyes, and a slender yet curvaceous figure—fueled her aspirations of becoming an actress. While she did not have a formal acting background, she often frequented the Hollywood Boulevard area, attending events and making her presence known in bars and nightclubs where she hoped to be discovered. Her soft-spoken nature and haunting beauty led many people in the city's social scene to take note of her.

At times, Elizabeth posed for photographs, and she was said to have met a few aspiring photographers who took shots of her for free, as they saw potential in her. She also reportedly spent time in the company of other young women who were similarly trying to break into Hollywood, including a few with minor acting credits. But Elizabeth's lack of professional acting experience was a significant barrier to her goals.

Unlike many of her contemporaries who were actively pursuing contracts with Hollywood studios or getting bit parts in films, Elizabeth was never able to land a major role. Some claim that she attended acting classes and took part in auditions, but there's little verifiable evidence to support these claims. What's known is that she became more known for her personal relationships, many of which were with men in the entertainment industry.

By the time of her death, Elizabeth had not achieved the fame she so desperately desired. However, she was still remembered by those who encountered her, not for any acting credits, but for her mysterious aura and unique personality. This created a paradox of sorts: while Elizabeth Short never became the famous actress she longed to be, the circumstances surrounding her death would ensure that her name became known far beyond the Hollywood circles she had hoped to break into.

## Relationships and Personal Struggles

Elizabeth Short's personal life was just as turbulent as her career aspirations. Throughout her time in Los Angeles, she became involved in a number of romantic relationships, some of which would later be scrutinized during the investigation into her death. Many of these relationships seemed to revolve around men with connections to Hollywood or the military, which was not unusual at the time, as the entertainment industry in Los Angeles was a social hub where people from all walks of life intersected.

One of the most significant relationships in Elizabeth's life was with a young man named Major Matthew Michael Gordon, a decorated U.S. Army soldier. They met in 1944, and their romance was intense but short-lived. Elizabeth and Matthew Gordon had a strong connection, but after he was sent to the Pacific theater during World War II, their relationship faced significant strain. When he was killed in a plane crash in 1945, Elizabeth was devastated. Many of her friends and acquaintances believed that this tragic event had a lasting emotional impact on her, and some even suggested that her heartbreak over Gordon's death may have contributed to her emotional instability in the years leading up to her murder.

In addition to her romantic entanglements, Elizabeth was known to have struggled with various emotional issues. She had spent some time in Florida before arriving in California, and during this time, she had been briefly hospitalized for psychological issues, though the specifics are unclear. Some accounts suggest that Elizabeth had bouts of depression, while others claim that she was simply a young woman disillusioned with her prospects in a city that promised much but delivered little. She reportedly sought comfort in the company of older men, some of whom were well-established in the Hollywood scene, but none of these relationships brought her the stability or success she sought.

Her reputation in Hollywood circles was not without its complications. Elizabeth was known to have dated men who had powerful connections, but none of these relationships led to a career in acting. In fact, many of the men she encountered were not interested in helping her professionally. Instead, they were more focused on her physical beauty and her ability to keep them entertained in social settings. This pattern repeated itself throughout her time in Los Angeles.

While many people remembered her as a beautiful and charming woman, those who were close to her often-described Elizabeth as being more vulnerable than she appeared. Her inability to achieve the fame she dreamed of, combined with the instability in her personal life, left her emotionally fragile. Friends and acquaintances would later remark that she seemed to lack a sense of direction and purpose, and that her tendency to form fleeting and sometimes unhealthy relationships was part of her struggle to find meaning in her life.

By late 1946, Elizabeth Short was living in a state of uncertainty. She had recently been involved with a few different men and had spent time in a few different residences, often moving between apartments and shared living spaces. She was also reportedly staying at a guest house in Los Angeles in the months leading up to her murder. Some accounts suggest that she may have been living in a more transient state during her final months, unsure of where her life was heading.

Her final days in Los Angeles were marked by a mix of loneliness, desperation, and a sense of helplessness. She may have begun to feel that the Hollywood dream was slipping further from her grasp. While she had not yet reached the fame she so desired, her tragic fate would ensure that her name would forever be linked to Hollywood, albeit in a way she could never have imagined.

# Part II: The Crime and Discovery

# Chapter 3

# The Final Days of Elizabeth Short

Elizabeth Short's final days remain shrouded in mystery, as the precise sequence of events leading up to her gruesome murder is largely speculative. By January 1947, Short had spent several months in Los Angeles, navigating the challenges of the city with dreams of becoming a movie star, but also facing the harsh realities of an uncertain future. Although she had been in and out of various relationships and had lived in temporary housing, it seemed that during the weeks before her death, Elizabeth's life had begun to take a more downward trajectory. It's in these final days that the truth about her life, her ambitions, and her relationships began to unravel, pieced together through witness statements, reports, and the tragic details of her murder.

## *Last Known Movements*

The last confirmed sighting of Elizabeth Short was on the evening of January 9, 1947. According to reports, she was last seen at the Biltmore Hotel in downtown Los Angeles, where she met with an acquaintance, Robert "Red" Manley, a 25-year-old married man. Manley, who later became one of the key individuals questioned by the police, said that he dropped short off at the hotel around 10:00 PM that evening. At that point, Short was known to be in good spirits, having made plans to meet a friend for breakfast the next morning. However, by the time the sun rose on January 15, 1947, Elizabeth Short had already been brutally murdered and left in a vacant lot.

Short's final days before her death remain somewhat murky, but there are a few known facts that offer a glimpse into the complexity of her life. After meeting with Manley, it is believed that Elizabeth spent the night at the Biltmore, but it is unclear whether she checked into a room or simply used the hotel as a resting place. Some reports suggest that she may have been seen in the hotel lobby the next morning, while others claim she was last seen conversing with a mysterious man, possibly a business contact or lover, the night before.

Over the course of the next few days, her whereabouts remain unaccounted for. According to several witnesses, Elizabeth Short was seen in different areas of Los Angeles, including Hollywood Boulevard and the vicinity of Sunset Boulevard. She was often described as walking alone, carrying an air of detachment and disillusionment, suggesting that she may have been struggling with the rejection she faced in Hollywood's tough entertainment industry. There are conflicting reports about whether she was meeting anyone or if she was simply wandering the city in search of work or companionship.

A key detail that emerges during this period is that Elizabeth had reportedly become involved in several brief romantic relationships, including one with a man named Mark Hansen, a nightclub owner who had briefly offered her financial support. However, it seems these relationships were neither stable nor long-lasting. Short's relationships, much like her time in Hollywood, were transient—based on promises of fame or survival but never offering her the stability or fulfillment she had hoped for.

## *Witnesses and Leads*

The discovery of Elizabeth Short's body on January 15, 1947, was made by a mother and her young daughter who were walking in the area. The girl spotted what she thought was a discarded mannequin lying in the vacant lot at 3925 South Norton Avenue, a street near Leimert Park, Los Angeles. Upon closer inspection, the mother realized it was a woman's body, severed and posed in a grotesque manner. The authorities were immediately notified, and within moments, the Los Angeles Police Department (LAPD) had cordoned off the scene.

At the crime scene, it was evident that Elizabeth Short had been subjected to a horrific and sadistic act. Her body had been severed in half at the waist, and the two halves were posed in a manner that suggested deliberate, calculated actions. In addition to this, her body was drained of blood, a detail that added to the eerie nature of the crime. Her face had been slashed, creating a grotesque "smile" on her features, and her body was left in a state of undress, with her clothing removed and arranged nearby. A key detail was that Elizabeth's body was cleaned, suggesting that the killer may have had medical knowledge or an unusual level of control over the crime scene.

The LAPD quickly launched a massive investigation into the circumstances of her death. Although they had no immediate leads, investigators began to sift through the accounts of those who had seen Elizabeth in the days leading up to her murder. Among the early suspects was Robert Manley, her last known acquaintance. Manley was questioned extensively but later cleared of any involvement in her death. Despite this, his role in the case remained significant, as he was one of the few people who had seen Short just before she disappeared.

As the investigation expanded, a number of witnesses came forward with varying accounts of having seen Elizabeth in different locations, including a possible meeting with a man who was described as tall and dark-haired. This individual, who has never been definitively identified, became a key figure in the investigation, with several theories suggesting that he could have been a stalker, a lover, or even the murderer himself. However, no conclusive evidence ever linked him to the crime.

The police also interviewed a number of people connected to Elizabeth's life, including those she had met through her brief stays at hotels, her acquaintances from Hollywood, and those who had known her during her earlier years in California. One of the most intriguing leads came from a hotel manager who described an interaction with Elizabeth shortly before her death. The manager stated that Short had approached him in a desperate manner, asking for a place to stay. Her request, made with a certain sense of urgency, suggested that Elizabeth was perhaps fleeing from someone or something. However, the manager later admitted that he was unsure whether the request was made out of fear or simply out of a desire to avoid returning to a relationship or situation she was attempting to escape.

## Life in Hollywood: The Shadow of a Starlet

Elizabeth Short's time in Hollywood, while relatively brief, was marked by both ambition and disillusionment. Like many young women who moved to Los Angeles during the post-World War II era, Elizabeth dreamed of becoming a film star. At 5'6" with striking features and long, dark hair, she possessed the physical attributes that many believed were suited for the silver screen. Despite these advantages, Elizabeth's dream of stardom never materialized in any substantial way.

Short's first arrival in Hollywood, in 1943, had been full of hope, but she soon found herself struggling with the harsh realities of the industry. She had no formal acting training, and while she was able to secure some minor roles and auditions, she found herself in the unfortunate position of being cast aside as just another hopeful starlet who failed to stand out. The reality of Hollywood was far more competitive and unforgiving than the fantasy she had envisioned. Elizabeth's name, while not immediately recognizable, would eventually be linked to one of the most infamous crimes in the city's history—her murder.

Despite a lack of formal acting success, Elizabeth did manage to catch the attention of several men in the industry, including wealthy individuals and aspiring film producers. However, none of these relationships seemed to offer her the career breakthrough she sought. She often found herself in temporary living situations, staying with friends or acquaintances, struggling financially, and always searching for the next opportunity. In this way, Elizabeth's life mirrored that of many aspiring actresses in the postwar era, yet it was marked by a sense of instability and uncertainty that set her apart from other hopefuls.

It's possible that Elizabeth's relationships with men and her lifestyle in Hollywood became more tumultuous as she realized that her dreams were unlikely to come true. Some reports suggest that she became more withdrawn and melancholier as time passed, occasionally indulging in alcohol and seeking comfort in brief affairs. She was not alone in her struggles—many young women moved to Hollywood in search of fame only to face rejection, exploitation, and a lack of genuine support. Elizabeth Short's life in Hollywood was, in many ways, defined by the difficulty of achieving the stardom she so desired, and it is clear that she was increasingly disillusioned by the city's empty promises.

## *The Shadow of a Starlet*

Hollywood, at the time, was a place of both glamour and danger, a city where dreams were made but where the gap between success and failure was often razor-thin. Elizabeth Short, with her dark beauty and ambition, was one of many young women who came to the city with aspirations of fame but ultimately faced the cruel indifference of an industry that consumed its most vulnerable. Her experiences in Hollywood, while unremarkable in the traditional sense of stardom, became symbolic of the fleeting nature of celebrity and the darker side of fame—the exploitation, the forgotten stories, and the men and women who were cast aside.

In this context, Elizabeth Short was not just a victim of a horrific crime but also a symbol of the many women who moved to Hollywood seeking fame, only to fall victim to an unforgiving system. Whether she was aware of the danger she was in or whether she became a target due to her vulnerability is still a matter of speculation. But what is clear is that her death, which would unfold as one of the most gruesome and baffling murders in history, was, in a sense, the final, tragic chapter in her story as an aspiring actress—a life cut short before her dreams could ever be realized.

# Chapter 4

# The Grisly Discovery

## The Discovery of the Body

On the morning of January 15, 1947, a disturbing discovery was made in a vacant lot at 3890 San Vicente Boulevard in Los Angeles. The area, located just a few miles west of the city's downtown, was known for its sparse, undeveloped land, offering a sense of isolation that still largely undeveloped, with scrubby lots and scattered, low-rise buildings. At approximately 10 a.m., a local housewife named Betty Bersinger was walking with her young daughter when they came across a grisly sight in the vacant lot. Initially, she thought the body lying on the ground was a discarded mannequin due to its pale, lifeless appearance and its oddly posed, disjointed limbs. As she got closer, however, she realized it was, in fact, the lifeless body of a woman.

The body was positioned in a stark and disturbing manner: the torso was severed at the waist, and the lower half of the body was several feet away from the upper half, creating an eerie image of dismemberment. The woman's mouth was cut into a grotesque smile, and her eyes were wide open, staring at nothing. Her skin was notably pale, and the body had been completely drained of blood, adding to the shocking nature of the scene.

The first instinct of the housewife, Betty Bersinger, was to flee the area and call the authorities. She hurried to a nearby phone booth, and within minutes, the police were dispatched to the scene. Officers from the Los Angeles Police Department (LAPD) arrived soon after, and the area was immediately cordoned off. What they found was not only a murder but a macabre crime scene that would intrigue the public and confound investigators for decades.

The body, later identified as Elizabeth Short, had been meticulously cleaned of blood, with the blood drained entirely from the corpse. This suggested a level of premeditation and care that baffled authorities. There were no obvious signs of a struggle or other physical evidence pointing to a killer who had acted in a moment of passion or violence. Instead, the crime seemed calculated and ritualistic, an aspect that would become central to the investigation as the case unfolded.

The disfigurement of Short's face was one of the most shocking aspects of the crime. Her mouth had been slit into a wide, grotesque smile, a feature that would give rise to the media's description of the crime scene as one of "Hollywood horror." This, along with other details of the body's mutilation, made the murder seem more than just a senseless act of violence—it suggested a deep-seated personal motive or perhaps a psychological component to the crime.

As the investigation began, authorities quickly realized the difficulty of solving a case as gruesome and bizarre as this one. The lack of immediate forensic clues and the strange condition of the body would challenge even the most seasoned detectives in Los Angeles.

## Early Investigations

Once the LAPD had secured the crime scene, the process of investigating the murder began in earnest. Detectives from the department's Homicide Bureau were assigned to the case, and they quickly began working through the details of Elizabeth Short's life, hoping to find any leads that might explain her tragic fate.

Early on, one of the most perplexing elements of the case was the complete lack of blood at the scene. It was as if the body had been carefully moved from another location. There was no evidence of a struggle, no bloodstains on the ground, and no indication that Short had been attacked where she was found. Her body had been cleaned and drained in a manner that suggested the killer had known exactly what he was doing. This unusual aspect of the crime suggested a level of sophistication and forethought, which would lead investigators to believe that the killer had planned the murder in advance.

However, despite the shocking nature of the crime, investigators found few clues at the scene. There were no apparent fingerprints or physical evidence that could lead them to a suspect. The only immediate clue came from the contents of Short's purse, which had been found nearby, abandoned but untouched. The purse contained some identification and personal effects, and through these items, investigators were able to confirm her identity. It was then that they learned of her connection to Los Angeles and her apparent dreams of becoming a Hollywood actress.

The discovery of Short's body sent shockwaves through the city of Los Angeles. At the time, the city was enjoying a golden age of Hollywood glamour, and the murder of a young woman with aspirations of stardom seemed all the more tragic. It wasn't long before reporters descended on the scene, and the press quickly picked up the story, sensationalizing every detail of the investigation. In the days that followed, the Black Dahlia murder would become front-page news, capturing the attention of the nation.

The LAPD, now under intense public pressure, threw all available resources into the investigation. Dozens of detectives, forensic experts, and even the FBI were called in to assist. But despite their efforts, the investigation soon ran into a series of dead ends. The lack of physical evidence and the bizarre nature of the crime made it extremely difficult to identify any leads. The case would soon become a challenge that even the most experienced investigators struggled to solve.

# The Crime Scene and Forensic Details

The crime scene where Elizabeth Short's body was discovered was as puzzling as it was horrifying. The vacant lot in which her body was found was relatively isolated, and it was not immediately clear why she had been left there. Investigators speculated that she had been killed elsewhere, possibly in a more secluded location, and her body had been transported to the lot after the murder. The method of disposal also raised questions. Why had the killer taken the time to carefully position the body and sever it in such a deliberate way?

Forensic analysis of the body revealed several chilling details. The most important and perplexing of these was the complete lack of blood. Short's body had been drained of blood; a detail that suggested the killer had not only taken great care in disposing of the body but had also gone to the trouble of performing this gruesome act of bloodletting. This unusual aspect of the case led authorities to speculate that the murderer might have some medical or surgical knowledge. It was an early indication that this crime was not just a random act of violence but one that involved a certain degree of planning and expertise.

Further forensic investigation revealed that Elizabeth Short had been dead for several days before her body was discovered. The cause of death was determined to be blunt force trauma to the head, likely delivered by a heavy object. There were also signs of severe trauma to the lower part of her body, including signs of dismemberment, but no clear indication of sexual assault. The manner in which her body had been disfigured suggested that the killer had deliberately targeted her face, cutting it with precision to create the infamous "glamour smile" that would forever be associated with her death.

One of the most unusual forensic details in the case was the lack of defensive wounds. Elizabeth Short had not fought back, nor did she appear to have struggled with her assailant. This raised questions about the nature of her death. Was she caught off guard? Was she incapacitated before the attack? Or had she been subdued in some other way?

Despite the bizarre and disturbing nature of the crime scene, the forensic investigation failed to provide any concrete leads. The killer had taken great care to remove evidence, and there was no way to determine exactly how or when Short had been murdered. The dismemberment of her body, as well as the careful positioning of the corpse, suggested that the killer was attempting to convey a message or perhaps to assert some level of control over the victim. The killer's surgical-like precision added a layer of mystery to the case, as it seemed to indicate that the crime was not an impulsive act, but a coldly calculated one.

As for the face of Elizabeth Short, the grotesque "glamour smile" that had been carved into her lips became one of the most enduring symbols of the case.

Was it the work of a sadistic killer? A symbol of something deeper, something psychological? Or was it, as some speculated, the twisted signature of a deranged mind who had wanted to humiliate or control his victim?

In the weeks that followed, the investigation intensified. Despite the lack of hard evidence, the police received numerous tips and reports from the public, some credible and others far-fetched. But none of these leads provided a breakthrough. As time passed, the case grew colder, and the Black Dahlia murder became yet another mysterious chapter in the annals of Los Angeles' dark criminal history. Yet, despite the mounting frustration among investigators, the public remained obsessed with the case, and it would continue to captivate the imagination of the media and the public for years to come.

# Chapter 5

# The Grisly Discovery 2

## *The Discovery of the Body*

On the morning of January 15, 1947, a discovery that would shake the city of Los Angeles and captivate the nation took place in a vacant lot on the corner of 39th Street and San Vicente Boulevard. This largely undeveloped, quiet neighborhood was about a mile from the heart of the city's thriving commercial district. At approximately 10 a.m., Betty Bersinger, a 37-year-old housewife, was walking with her young daughter when they came upon the body of a woman lying in the dirt. At first, Bersinger thought it was a mannequin—its pale, lifeless appearance, coupled with the way it lay unnaturally in the open, led her to this assumption. However, a closer inspection soon revealed the chilling reality.

The body was that of a woman, and it was apparent that she had been brutally murdered. The gruesome nature of the discovery immediately sent shockwaves through the community. The woman's body was severely mutilated and posed in a bizarre and shocking manner: her body had been severed at the waist, and her limbs spread out symmetrically, almost as though placed deliberately in a grotesque pose. The face, meanwhile, was ravaged—her mouth had been slashed into a grotesque smile, and her eyes had been removed.

Bersinger, realizing the enormity of what she had stumbled upon, quickly ran to a nearby phone to call the police. Within minutes, officers from the Los Angeles Police Department (LAPD) arrived at the scene and cordoned off the area. They immediately began to investigate, but it quickly became clear that this was no ordinary crime.

The victim's body was quickly identified as Elizabeth Short, though her name would not become widely known until the media picked up the case. At the time, Short had been in Los Angeles for several months, and authorities soon discovered that she had been living a transient lifestyle. Her body, however, would become the centerpiece of an investigation that would span years, create countless media headlines, and give rise to numerous theories and suspects.

## *Early Investigations*

The LAPD's investigation into the Black Dahlia murder began in earnest shortly after the body was discovered. Officers immediately combed the crime scene, looking for clues that might point to the identity of the killer. However, they quickly realized that the circumstances surrounding the murder were highly unusual, and any attempt to solve the crime would be fraught with difficulty.

One of the first issues facing the police was the absence of any obvious witnesses. The lot where the body was discovered was secluded, and no one had reported hearing anything unusual the previous night. The surrounding area was residential, but it seemed that the crime had been committed in the dead of night or early morning, well before any neighbors were up and about. The lack of eyewitnesses meant that police would have to rely heavily on forensic evidence, witness statements from people who had known Short, and any leads that might be uncovered in the days and weeks that followed.

The LAPD soon learned that Elizabeth Short had been living in various places in Los Angeles, including short stints in motels and apartments. However, she had no permanent address, and this added to the difficulty of piecing together the final days of her life. Her personal history appeared to be marked by a string of failed relationships, financial struggles, and a growing sense of isolation, though no one could confirm her whereabouts or who she had been associating with in the days leading up to her death.

Investigators immediately turned their attention to her personal life, interviewing friends, acquaintances, and anyone who might have had any knowledge of her final days. One key lead came from a woman named Jean French, who had last seen Elizabeth on the evening of

January 14, 1947. According to French, Elizabeth had been in high spirits and had even made plans to meet up again the following day. This seemed to suggest that Short's death had been sudden and unexpected, adding to the mystery of her violent demise.

The initial investigation into Elizabeth's death quickly took on a sense of urgency. The LAPD was under intense public scrutiny, as the murder of a young woman in the city was the kind of event that demanded quick resolution. The fact that the crime was particularly grisly, and that Short had been a somewhat public figure in her own right, only fueled the media's growing interest in the case. Journalists from newspapers across the country, especially the *Los Angeles Examiner* and *Los Angeles Times*, began to cover the crime in vivid detail, turning Elizabeth Short into an object of public fascination.

## The Crime Scene and Forensic Details

The condition of Elizabeth Short's body was both shocking and perplexing. The body had been severed at the waist with great precision, and her body appeared to have been drained of blood, making it difficult for investigators to establish the exact cause of death. The gruesome dismemberment, combined with the unnatural placement of the body, suggested that whoever had killed Elizabeth had some degree of anatomical knowledge. While many speculated that the mutilations could have been the work of a psychopath, some suggested that the killer might have had experience in the medical field, or even a surgical background.

One of the most disturbing aspects of the crime scene was the condition of Elizabeth's face. Her mouth had been slashed open in a "smile" that has since become one of the most iconic and chilling aspects of the case. The expression, now forever associated with the Black Dahlia murder, was made with a deep, jagged cut from one ear to the other, creating an eerily wide grin. This was widely believed to be a deliberate act, intended to make the victim appear more grotesque and to leave a lasting impression on anyone who would come across her body. Some investigators suggested that the killer might have been attempting to convey some sort of symbolic message with the smile, though its meaning remains elusive.

The fact that Short's eyes had been removed also added to the macabre nature of the crime. The removal of the eyes is a detail that continues to be debated among crime experts and criminologists. Some have speculated that the killer may have taken the eyes as a trophy, while others believe the removal was a way to further degrade the victim and further dehumanize her. Regardless of the motive, it was clear that the killer had taken steps to make the crime even more unsettling and grotesque.

Despite the brutal nature of the crime, there was little evidence left behind that could be used to identify the killer. There were no fingerprints, and no signs of struggle at the scene. Elizabeth Short had not been sexually assaulted, which led many to question the motive behind the murder. The absence of any obvious motive and the calculated nature of the crime led some experts to suggest that the killer was a psychopath, someone who had planned the murder meticulously without any clear reason.

The forensic analysis of the body also raised some important questions. The time of death was estimated to be sometime in the early hours of January 15, 1947, though the exact time was difficult to pinpoint due to the lack of physical evidence, such as blood spatter or defensive wounds. Investigators were unable to determine if Elizabeth had been alive when she was severed at the waist, though the careful nature of the dissection made it appear as though the act had been carried out with some degree of precision.

While police combed the crime scene and searched for physical evidence, they also attempted to reconstruct Elizabeth Short's final movements. The lack of any clear physical evidence or immediate witnesses led them to focus on her past. Her life before the murder was marked by a series of false leads, conflicting reports, and little information about the people she had been close to in her final days. The killer's ability to leave so few clues was one of the factors that would keep the case from being solved for decades, making it one of the most notorious unsolved murders in American history.

# Investigative Challenges and Media Frenzy

In the days and weeks following the discovery of the body, the investigation into the Black Dahlia murder quickly became a media sensation. The press, hungry for any scrap of information, painted Elizabeth Short as a tragic victim whose dreams of Hollywood stardom had been shattered in the most horrific way possible. The media frenzy, coupled with widespread public interest, only heightened the pressure on the LAPD to solve the case quickly.

As the investigation deepened, the authorities found themselves facing numerous obstacles. The lack of physical evidence, the absence of witnesses, and the peculiar nature of the crime made it difficult to piece together a clear timeline of events. The press continued to speculate wildly, publishing stories that often included sensational and unverified details, such as rumors of Elizabeth's alleged sexual relationships, her troubled past, and even possible connections to organized crime.

Though the LAPD's investigation continued, the case remained unsolved, and as the years passed, the mystery of the Black Dahlia murder would become even more enigmatic. The media continued to report on new developments, while amateur sleuths and self-proclaimed experts offered their own theories about who might have committed the crime. The discovery of Elizabeth Short's body was just the beginning of a story that would capture the public's attention for decades to come.

Despite the challenges faced by the LAPD and the overwhelming public interest, the investigation into the Black Dahlia murder would prove to be one of the most complicated and confounding in the annals of criminal history. The crime scene itself, with its grisly details and forensic anomalies, only added to the sense of mystery, and as the years turned into decades, the case would remain open and unresolved, haunting the streets of Los Angeles and inspiring countless theories, books, films, and documentaries.

In the end, the grisly discovery of Elizabeth Short's body marked the beginning of an investigation that would span years, create public fascination, and leave behind a legacy of questions that have never been answered.

# Part III: The Investigation

# Chapter 6

# The Police Investigation

When the mutilated body of Elizabeth Short was discovered in the vacant lot on January 15, 1947, the Los Angeles Police Department (LAPD) was immediately thrust into a high-profile investigation that would be both challenging and bewildering. The crime scene, with its shocking brutality, pointed to a murder of horrific proportions, but it also provided few clear clues that would help law enforcement determine who was responsible.

At first glance, the discovery appeared to be the work of a serial killer due to the highly ritualistic nature of the crime. Elizabeth's body had been severed at the waist, and her corpse had been drained of blood. Her mouth had been slashed from ear to ear, giving her a grotesque "smile" — a horrific feature that would later become the hallmark of the Black Dahlia case. Her body was positioned in a way that seemed to suggest the killer wanted it to be found. While the gruesome nature of the crime suggested a personal vendetta, or perhaps the work of a deranged mind, there were no obvious fingerprints or physical evidence left at the scene that could directly link any suspect to the murder.

The LAPD, faced with one of the most disturbing crimes in the city's history, launched an intense investigation. Detectives quickly combed through Short's personal history, speaking to friends, acquaintances, and those who had crossed paths with her in her brief time in Los Angeles. They attempted to reconstruct her final days, hoping to uncover some clue that would lead them to a killer. But as the weeks passed without any significant leads, the case grew even more perplexing.

One of the first challenges faced by investigators was Short's elusive nature. While they discovered that she had arrived in Los Angeles in 1943, Elizabeth's life was marked by instability and transience. She had lived in various boarding houses, apartments, and even with friends during her time in California. She often moved from place to place, rarely staying in one spot for long. As such, there was little evidence of a stable lifestyle or any permanent connections that could easily lead the police to the perpetrator.

Despite the initial lack of physical evidence, the LAPD turned their attention to the numerous people who had crossed paths with Short during her time in Hollywood. One of the first individuals to be questioned was a man named Robert "Red" Manley, a car salesman who had reportedly been seen with Short in the days leading up to her murder. Manley, who would later become one of the more high-profile figures associated with the case, was initially considered a prime suspect. However, after being interrogated for several days, he was eventually cleared of involvement in the crime. His alibi and lack of physical evidence linking him to the crime scene allowed him to walk free, although the media would continue to scrutinize his role in Short's life and death.

## *Early Suspects and Leads*

As the investigation into Elizabeth Short's death continued, a number of suspects were considered, each bringing with them their own complexities and challenges for the investigators. One of the most notable aspects of the case was the multitude of theories that emerged, ranging from professional killers to vengeful lovers. The LAPD was inundated with tips, confessions, and leads from the public, many of which seemed to stem from either a desire for fame or the inherent intrigue of the case. But despite the flood of information, the police remained unable to form a clear theory about what happened to Elizabeth Short.

One early suspect was a man named George Hodel, a prominent Los Angeles physician who was rumored to have had connections to a number of unsolved crimes in the city. Hodel was known for his eccentric behavior, and he had been linked to several women during the time he was under investigation. His suspicious behavior, including his strange remarks about the murder and his connection to the Los Angeles area at the time of the crime, made him an early person of interest.

However, despite a number of circumstantial details, no conclusive evidence linked Hodel to the murder. Furthermore, the LAPD was not able to secure enough physical evidence or solid witnesses to charge him with the crime. Hodel would later become a figure of interest in connection with other unsolved murders in the area, but in the case of the Black Dahlia, he was never formally charged.

Another lead came in the form of a letter sent to the Los Angeles Examiner, which arrived shortly after the body was discovered. The letter, postmarked in Los Angeles, was written in a strange, almost cryptic tone, and it contained a chilling message: "Here is Dahlia's belongings. Let me know if I can help." Along with the letter, a small package was enclosed that contained Elizabeth Short's personal items, including her social security card and identification. The letter sent to the newspaper was a chilling clue that suggested the killer wanted to remain involved in the case, feeding the police false hope that they were getting closer to solving the crime.

The letter and package were analyzed by the LAPD, but again, the leads went cold. Though they were able to determine the letter's authenticity, no fingerprints or other evidence could be extracted from it. The case would go on to be defined by this frustrating cycle of dead ends, misdirection, and false hope, as law enforcement struggled to make any substantial progress.

One of the most unsettling aspects of the investigation was the continued influx of false confessions. Individuals, often with mental health issues or seeking attention, began to call the police, claiming to have information about the murder or even to have been responsible for it themselves. In some cases, these confessions were so detailed that they seemed legitimate. But after thorough investigation, each of these leads proved to be false, leaving the police even more frustrated and unsure of where to turn next. This phenomenon would continue throughout the investigation, making it even more difficult for detectives to separate the real leads from the false ones.

## Media Influence on the Case

The media's influence on the Black Dahlia case cannot be overstated. As details of the murder emerged, newspapers, radio stations, and later, television, became obsessed with the mystery surrounding Elizabeth Short's death. The grisly nature of the crime, coupled with the mystery of her life and her sudden, untimely demise, made for sensational news that captivated the public.

The Los Angeles Examiner, in particular, played a pivotal role in shaping the narrative surrounding the murder. The newspaper's editor, James Richardson, was one of the first to publicize the shocking details of the crime, including the discovery of Elizabeth's mutilated body and the strange letter that had been sent to the newspaper. The sensational nature of the story catapulted the Black Dahlia case into the national spotlight, and soon, media outlets across the country were reporting on the murder.

The press, however, was not just reporting on the facts. They began to create a narrative around Elizabeth Short that was as much about speculation and rumor as it was about actual investigation. Headlines painted her as a femme fatale, a tragic starlet who had been caught in the seedy underworld of Hollywood. Her image in the press was one of mystery and allure, and many newspapers and magazines began to fabricate details about her life, her relationships, and her tragic end.

In some cases, the media seemed to take on an almost investigative role, publishing articles and conjectures about potential suspects, motives, and the identity of the killer. They fed into the public's fascination with the case, amplifying the mystery and fueling the sensationalism surrounding the Black Dahlia.

While the media's influence helped keep the case in the public eye, it also had a detrimental effect. The intense coverage of the crime, the widespread speculation, and the public's constant engagement with the case created a pressure cooker environment that would make it harder for the LAPD to solve the crime. Investigators were constantly dealing with misdirection, false leads, and a flood of information from self-proclaimed experts and amateur detectives, many of whom were only interested in the case because of the media circus it had become.

Moreover, Elizabeth Short's tragic life and death were reduced to a story fit for tabloid fodder. The public and the media alike became obsessed with the sensational aspects of her life, turning her into an icon of both fascination and tragedy, rather than focusing on the real, heartbreaking elements of her story. In this way, the media's coverage of the Black Dahlia case both illuminated and obscured the truth.

## *The Search for a Killer*

Despite months of relentless investigation, the LAPD's search for the Black Dahlia killer would remain elusive. While there were many theories, suspects, and leads, the case remained unsolved. New information would surface sporadically, but it rarely provided enough detail to make any significant breakthrough.

The lack of concrete evidence, combined with the overwhelming number of false confessions and the media frenzy, made it increasingly difficult for detectives to focus on a single suspect. But as the investigation stretched on, new theories began to emerge. Some believed the killer was a local resident, while others pointed to the possibility of a deranged outsider. The LAPD was divided over whether the crime had been committed by a serial killer or whether it was a one-off, deeply personal act of violence.

In the years following Elizabeth Short's death, the Black Dahlia case would continue to captivate the public imagination. The search for her killer — and the mystery of her life — would persist as one of the most enduring elements of Los Angeles' dark, mysterious past.

# Chapter 7

## Public and Media Response

### The "Black Dahlia" Media Frenzy

The discovery of Elizabeth Short's body on January 15, 1947, sent shockwaves through Los Angeles, but the subsequent media frenzy transformed her tragic death into an international sensation. This was long before the digital age, but even in the mid-20th century, the press played an outsized role in shaping public perception. The murder of Elizabeth Short — or "The Black Dahlia," as she would soon be dubbed — gripped the public imagination, fueled by the press's sensationalized portrayal of the crime.

As news of the discovery spread, newspapers across Los Angeles and the nation quickly seized on the gruesome details of the crime. They highlighted the severity of Short's mutilation — her body severed in two and drained of blood, with a grotesque smile carved into her face and other signs of surgical precision in the dissection. This gruesome image captivated readers and left many of them horrified, but it also fueled morbid curiosity. The media was quick to exploit the mystery surrounding the case, repeatedly emphasizing Short's enigmatic persona, her supposed "dark past," and her dreams of stardom in Hollywood.

One of the most notable early contributors to the media frenzy was the **Los Angeles Examiner**, a prominent local tabloid. The paper's editor, **James Richardson**, who would later become famous for his role in stoking public interest in the case, quickly adopted the term "Black Dahlia" to describe the victim. The nickname, inspired by the 1946 film *The Blue Dahlia*, was meant to evoke a sense of mystery and allure. The paper ran sensationalized headlines about the "Dahlia's" murder, leading to an immediate and overwhelming public fascination.

As the case developed, newspapers published lurid and often unsubstantiated details, some of which were either fabricated or sourced from unreliable informants. Stories about Elizabeth Short's alleged promiscuity, her relationships with men, and her life as a struggling actress became major points of focus. These details helped perpetuate a narrative of a beautiful, ambitious young woman who had fallen victim to the underbelly of Hollywood, a city known for its excesses, broken dreams, and darker realities.

Media outlets also played a major role in spreading photographs of Elizabeth Short, often publishing highly stylized and posed pictures of her, as well as images from her life in Los Angeles. The press romanticized her as a "fallen starlet," drawing comparisons between her tragic end and the lives of other Hollywood actresses whose careers had faltered. The public was captivated by the image of Short as a starlet on the brink of fame, whose promising future was cut short by a grisly fate. The media focused on her good looks, emphasizing her role as a beautiful woman who was inexplicably thrust into the world of fame, only to meet a tragic and violent end.

Though there were few real leads or solid evidence in the case, the media's voracious appetite for information fueled the public's obsession with the mystery. As the story gained momentum, countless theories, rumors, and speculations about the identity of the killer began to circulate. Journalists and columnists turned the case into a sensational drama that was impossible to ignore. This media coverage — often exaggerating details and spreading misinformation — had a profound impact on the course of the investigation and would ultimately shape the narrative surrounding the Black Dahlia murder for decades to come.

## *Public Perception and Sensationalism*

As the media frenzy around the Black Dahlia murder grew, public perception became distorted by sensationalism and the relentless desire for new and shocking details. In the wake of such a brutal crime, many people were drawn into the case not just because of its gruesome nature, but because of the larger-than-life narrative that had been built around Elizabeth Short. She was no longer just a young woman who had been murdered — she became a symbol of tragedy, a cautionary tale about the dangers of Hollywood, and a figure to be discussed and dissected by the public.

One of the most striking elements of public perception was the way in which Elizabeth Short's personal life was framed by the press and, in turn, by the public. The media's focus on her beauty, her alleged promiscuity, and her mysterious past played into the idea of the "fallen woman," a trope often used in sensational crimes to create an air of moral judgment. People began to imagine Elizabeth not as a person, but as a symbol of something darker — the innocent woman undone by the corrupt world of Hollywood. The public was led to believe that she had somehow invited her own death through her lifestyle, whether real or imagined.

Public reaction to the murder was also strongly influenced by the racial and gender dynamics at play. The press's coverage of Short's life and death reinforced certain stereotypes about women in the entertainment industry. While Short was being painted as a beautiful, but tragic figure, there was also a sense of moral outrage directed at her. Her alleged relationships with men were exaggerated, often painting her as an ambitious woman whose pursuit of fame made her a victim of sexual violence and exploitation.

The sensationalism surrounding the Black Dahlia case extended beyond her personal life and into the very nature of the crime itself. The brutal and seemingly surgical nature of the murder, the dismemberment of the body, and the mysterious circumstances surrounding Short's death led to rampant speculation that the killer was someone highly intelligent, possibly even a medical professional. The crime was so shocking, so meticulously executed, that it seemed to defy ordinary explanation. The public fascination with this "perfect crime" added an element of intrigue that kept the case in the public eye for years.

Rumors also played a significant role in shaping public perception. With no definitive answers from the police, conspiracy theories began to emerge. Some believed that Elizabeth Short's death was part of a larger conspiracy involving the Hollywood elite, while others speculated that she had been murdered by a deranged stalker or a jealous lover. These theories played into the public's desire for a narrative that was not only sensational but also larger than life. The lack of concrete evidence or closure only fueled these wild speculations.

As the weeks turned into months and then years, the public's initial shock and fascination began to transform into a sense of frustration. People became obsessed with finding answers to the mystery, but the more they speculated, the further the case seemed to drift into uncertainty. The killer remained at large, and with each passing year, the case became a symbol of unresolved darkness, a haunting reminder of the complexities and tragedies that lay hidden beneath the glamorous surface of Hollywood.

# How the Case Captivated America

The Black Dahlia murder is often described as a quintessential American crime — one that reflects the darker side of the American dream. Elizabeth Short's tragic death, combined with the media's sensationalized portrayal of the case, captivated not just Los Angeles, but the entire nation. The case became a symbol of the way in which crime, celebrity, and societal fascination with scandal are intertwined in the fabric of American culture.

The Black Dahlia murder was unique in that it occurred during a time when American culture was becoming increasingly fixated on both celebrity and crime. The 1940s was the era of film noir, a genre known for its dark, morally ambiguous characters and gritty depictions of crime. In many ways, the Black Dahlia case seemed straight out of a noir film. The beautiful, vulnerable woman, the dark city of Los Angeles, the mysterious killer — all the elements of a classic crime story were present. But in this case, the story was real, and the outcome was far more horrifying.

At the time of the murder, America was also experiencing a post-World War II boom in mass media, particularly in the realm of television and newspapers. The rapid expansion of the media created a perfect storm for public fascination with crime stories. The Black Dahlia murder became a topic of conversation across the country, transcending Los Angeles and reaching into living rooms via newspapers, radio, and eventually, television. Stories about Elizabeth Short's life and death filled the pages of newspapers from coast to coast. People across the United States, who had never met Elizabeth Short or even been to Los Angeles, were drawn into the case by the vivid imagery and sensational reporting.

In a way, the Black Dahlia case prefigured the way modern crime stories — particularly those involving celebrities — would unfold in the media. It demonstrated how a tragic event could quickly be transformed into a cultural obsession, where the details of a person's life were picked apart for public consumption. In many ways, the case also highlighted the growing trend of true crime stories as a form of mass entertainment. Elizabeth Short's life, death, and the mystery of her killer would be the subject of books, films, documentaries, and countless other retellings, further embedding her story into the national consciousness.

The fascination with the Black Dahlia was not just about the crime itself, but about what it represented. It symbolized the intersection of fame, violence, and the dark undercurrents of American society. The allure of the case lay in its mysterious, tragic nature, and its reflection of the seductive and often dangerous world of Hollywood. The Black Dahlia murder, with its macabre details and its unresolved mystery, became a symbol of both the promise and the peril of fame, and for many, it remains one of the most compelling and disturbing crime stories in American history.

# Chapter 8

# Theories and Suspects

## *A Gallery of Potential Suspects*

Over the years, the Black Dahlia case has seen an array of individuals emerge as potential suspects, ranging from people connected to Elizabeth Short's personal life to notorious criminals, as well as a host of more obscure figures. Despite exhaustive investigations and numerous leads, the identity of Elizabeth Short's murderer remains a mystery. In this section, we will explore some of the more prominent suspects in the case, some of whom have been named by the public, the media, or even law enforcement, while others have entered the realm of speculation and conspiracy.

### 1. George Hodel

One of the most well-known and controversial suspects in the Black Dahlia case is Dr. George Hodel, a wealthy Los Angeles physician. Hodel's name has been frequently linked to the crime, particularly due to the persistence of crime writer and former LAPD detective

Steve Hodel, who spent years investigating his own father's potential involvement.

Hodel, a respected doctor, was a man of complex character. His personal life was marked by scandal and intrigue, including allegations of sexual misconduct and a tumultuous relationship with his daughter, Tamar. However, it was his connection to the Black Dahlia case that brought him the most infamy.

In 1949, just two years after the murder, Hodel was named as a suspect by the LAPD, although there was never enough evidence to charge him. His name resurfaced in the early 2000s when Steve Hodel began publicly claiming that his father had been the murderer. The elder Hodel had connections to the scene of the crime—he owned property near the area where Elizabeth Short's body was discovered, and a 1947 photograph purportedly showed him in the company of a woman who resembled Short.

Steve Hodel's theory was bolstered by the suggestion that his father was a suspect in several other unsolved murders, including the "Dahlia-like" killing of an aspiring actress named Jean Spangler. While there is no conclusive evidence linking George Hodel to Short's death, his reputation and connections continue to make him a prominent figure in theories about the case.

## 2. Richard "Dick" Anderson

Another suspect in the Black Dahlia case is Richard "Dick" Anderson, a former LAPD officer and a well-known figure in the Los Angeles underworld. Anderson was one of the many individuals who came forward after Elizabeth Short's death, suggesting he had been in contact with her in the days leading up to her murder. Anderson claimed that he had an affair with Short shortly before her death, and while he was never formally accused of the crime, his proximity to Short and his mysterious background made him a person of interest.

The allegations surrounding Anderson were not entirely substantiated, but they added a layer of intrigue to the investigation. Some speculate that Anderson may have been involved in criminal activities that could have contributed to Short's death, particularly in light of the fact that some believed she was on the brink of exposing a significant Los Angeles sex ring.

### 3. The "Man in the Black Suit"

Throughout the years, numerous other suspects have been proposed, including the enigmatic "Man in the Black Suit," a figure described by several witnesses who claimed to have seen a man with a dark suit and hat near the scene of the crime shortly before Elizabeth Short's body was discovered. This vague but haunting description became one of the most discussed elements of the case.

Some investigators suggest that the man may have been involved in Short's death, either as an accomplice or even as the murderer himself. However, there has never been any concrete evidence to confirm the existence of such a man, and the witness testimony remains contradictory.

## 4. Walter Bayley

Walter Bayley, a retired surgeon, was named as a suspect by multiple individuals who were close to the case. Bayley's name resurfaced in the 1970s after several pieces of circumstantial evidence linked him to the Black Dahlia murder. According to a former LAPD detective, Bayley's wife was reportedly familiar with Short and may have been involved in a dispute with her shortly before the murder. Bayley's background as a physician and his access to surgical tools, which could have been used to mutilate Short's body, further raised suspicions.

Bayley's connection to the crime, however, remains speculative. While some proponents of the theory argue that his background made him a plausible suspect, there is no concrete evidence to definitively link him to the murder.

## 5. Other Suspects

Over the years, the list of suspects has expanded to include various individuals, some of whom were connected to Short's social circle, including lovers, acquaintances, and those who may have known her from her time in Hollywood. These individuals range from disgruntled lovers to potential serial killers, but none have been conclusively identified as Short's killer.

In addition to the suspects mentioned, other notable individuals have been suggested, including several who had criminal backgrounds, such as notorious gangsters or individuals involved in the Los Angeles criminal underworld. Speculation also exists that the killer may have been a disturbed individual with no direct connection to Short but who targeted her due to her beauty, vulnerability, or connection to the entertainment industry.

While these suspects all play significant roles in the case's lore, none have been definitively proven to be Elizabeth Short's murderer, and the identity of the true killer remains elusive.

## The Most Prominent Theories

Given the high-profile nature of the Black Dahlia case and the many suspects involved, numerous theories have emerged over the years to explain the events surrounding Elizabeth Short's murder. Some are based on circumstantial evidence, others on psychological analysis or the patterns of serial killers in the post-war period. Here are some of the most prominent theories:

### 1. The Serial Killer Theory

One of the most widely discussed theories is that Elizabeth Short's death was the work of a serial killer. Proponents of this theory point to the brutality and precision of the murder as indicative of someone with a clear pattern or a history of violent behavior. The idea that Short may have been a "chosen victim" who fit a specific psychological profile was explored by criminologists who examined her murder in the broader context of other unsolved crimes during that time period.

Some have suggested that the murderer may have been an unrecognized serial killer who targeted other women in Los Angeles, but whose crimes went unnoticed until the Black Dahlia case drew national attention. This theory has gained further traction with the identification of other potential "Dahlia-like" murders, including the aforementioned Jean Spangler case, which shares several eerie similarities to Short's death.

## 2. The Hollywood Conspiracy Theory

Another prominent theory is that Elizabeth Short's murder was tied to a conspiracy involving Hollywood elites. Some believe that her dreams of stardom may have led her into the dangerous world of Hollywood's dark side—where powerful men exploited young actresses, often with tragic consequences. Short's alleged involvement with several men who were prominent in the industry and her apparent connections to Hollywood's more sordid underbelly have led some to speculate that her murder was a way to silence her.

This theory also suggests that Short's death was not random but part of a larger, organized effort to prevent her from exposing the inner workings of the entertainment industry. While no direct evidence supports this claim, the Hollywood conspiracy theory remains one of the most persistent and sensationalized ideas about the Black Dahlia case.

### 3. The Love Triangle Theory

Some believe that the murder was the result of a love triangle or a relationship gone wrong. Elizabeth Short was reportedly involved with several men, including army servicemen, as well as wealthy individuals who were intrigued by her beauty and aspirations. The theory suggests that her murder was driven by jealousy, anger, or revenge—perhaps by a lover or a man spurned by her affections. This idea posits that a jealous lover or husband could have committed the crime in a fit of rage, though it would have required a degree of premeditation and sadistic intent to carry out the brutal mutilations that followed.

### 4. The "Surgical Precision" Theory

Given the nature of Elizabeth Short's murder, many have speculated that her killer may have had medical or surgical training. The manner in which her body was dismembered, with precise cuts made to the abdomen and the removal of organs, suggested to some investigators that the killer had knowledge of human anatomy. This theory focuses on the idea that Short's murderer was a physician, surgeon, or someone with access to surgical tools—possibly explaining why George Hodel, a doctor, became a key suspect in the case.

This theory, while speculative, has gained significant attention over the years due to the chilling accuracy of the mutilations and the apparent lack of remorse exhibited by the killer. Many believe that such a meticulous crime required a certain level of expertise, which a trained medical professional would have had.

## Expert Opinions and Hypotheses

Criminologists and forensic experts have long weighed in on the Black Dahlia case, providing various analyses of the murder and the circumstances surrounding it. Expert opinions tend to vary widely, as no one theory or suspect has been definitively proven.

### 1. Psychological Analysis of the Killer

Experts in criminal psychology have suggested that Elizabeth Short's killer may have been a highly disturbed individual with a history of violence or mental illness. The extreme mutilation of Short's body, along with the fact that the killer displayed no apparent remorse or guilt, points to someone who was either highly sadistic or suffering from severe psychological issues.

Some psychological profiles of the killer emphasize the idea that he may have been a "repressed" individual, possibly someone living a double life, and that the murder represented a release of pent-up anger or frustration. The careful planning of the crime and the precise execution of the murder suggest that the killer may have had a deep need to assert control or power, which may align with common traits found in serial killers.

## 2. The Involvement of Multiple Killers

Another theory that has gained traction over the years is the idea that Elizabeth Short's murder was not the work of a single individual, but rather the result of a coordinated effort by multiple perpetrators. While there is no concrete evidence to support the theory of multiple killers, some aspects of the crime scene and the circumstances surrounding Short's murder have led certain investigators and theorists to speculate about the possibility of more than one person being involved.

One of the primary pieces of evidence that fuels this theory is the sheer brutality of the murder. The methodical and calculated nature of the crime — the severing of the victim's body in two, the draining of her blood, and the precise arrangement of her body — has led some experts to suggest that it could be the work of a team of killers who were able to work in tandem to execute the crime with precision.

Additionally, there are those who suggest that Elizabeth Short's murder was not the work of a single "lone wolf" killer but was part of a larger pattern of killings, possibly even a series of murders committed by a group of people. The theory of multiple perpetrators would also potentially explain the lack of direct evidence linking any one suspect to the crime. If more than one person was involved, it could have been much harder for investigators to connect the dots or find a single suspect who could be linked to the murder. Some even theorize that the killers might have had an insider knowledge of Short's habits, allowing them to abduct her and transport her without arousing suspicion.

This theory remains highly controversial. It's not universally accepted, and it remains difficult to separate fact from conjecture in the murky waters of this particular theory. But it continues to be explored, especially by those who are convinced that the nature of the crime could not have been carried out by a single individual.

### 3. The "Copycat Killer" Theory

Another fascinating theory surrounding the Black Dahlia murder is the notion that Short's killer was inspired or influenced by previous high-profile murders. This theory proposes that her murder might not have been entirely original, but rather that the killer was attempting to replicate or emulate a prior, notorious crime.

In this case, the idea is that Elizabeth Short's murderer may have had a specific interest in other famous unsolved crimes, perhaps drawing inspiration from them in terms of the brutality and spectacle of the crime. One notable example is the infamous "Torso Murderer" who had been active in the early 1930s in the Midwest, most notably in the Cleveland area, where a series of gruesome dismemberments and decapitations had occurred. These murders, though geographically distant, shared similar characteristics with the Black Dahlia case, leading some to speculate that the murderer might have seen himself as a "copycat" following a long-established pattern of violence.

The theory of a "copycat killer" could explain the deliberate and theatrical nature of the Black Dahlia murder, with its over-the-top brutality, the display of the body, and the meticulous dissection. Some have also pointed to the public nature of the crime — occurring in a public space and becoming an immediate media sensation — as a clue that the killer was driven by the desire for notoriety. It's possible that whoever killed Elizabeth Short saw her murder as a way to mimic or surpass the notoriety of earlier unsolved cases, believing that such a gruesome and public murder would bring them attention and infamy.

The idea of a copycat killer also brings into focus the role of the media in shaping the nature of the crime. The coverage of the Black Dahlia case, with its sensational headlines, extensive press coverage, and public obsession, might have set a dangerous precedent for other criminals. As the media frenzy surrounding the Black Dahlia intensified, it could have inadvertently created an environment where other killers felt compelled to replicate the crime in order to gain the same level of attention.

Though it is difficult to draw a direct link between the Black Dahlia murder and any earlier crimes, the possibility of a copycat scenario continues to be a compelling angle in understanding the motivations of Elizabeth Short's killer. However, it remains an unsolved and speculative element in the overall investigation.

## 4. The Zodiac Killer Connection

Perhaps one of the most enduring, yet controversial, theories involve a potential link between the Black Dahlia murder and the infamous Zodiac Killer, a serial killer who terrorized Northern California during the late 1960s and early 1970s. Although the Zodiac Killer's known killings occurred two decades after Elizabeth Short's murder, some believe that the two cases share striking similarities, including the killer's penchant for publicizing their crimes and sending cryptic messages to the media.

The idea that the Zodiac Killer could have been involved in the Black Dahlia murder is speculative and based on a combination of circumstantial evidence, psychological profiles, and the killer's infamous desire for attention. The Zodiac Killer, like the person responsible for Short's death, seemed to thrive on public attention and reveled in the media coverage of their crimes. Both killers left taunting clues, with Zodiac sending cryptic letters to the press, and the Black Dahlia murderer sending letters and photographs to the media after Short's death.

There are also similarities in the modus operandi of both killers. The Zodiac Killer, like Short's murderer, often performed meticulous, ritualistic killings, taking great care in how he disposed of the bodies of his victims. The murder of Elizabeth Short also involved precise dissection, as well as an element of theater, with the body posed and displayed in a way that suggested an obsession with making a statement. While the Zodiac Killer's crimes were often performed in isolated areas, his messages and behavior pointed to a deeper desire for recognition and the exploitation of the public's fear and fascination.

Despite these similarities, there is no direct evidence linking the Zodiac Killer to the Black Dahlia murder. The idea that they are connected has been widely criticized by law enforcement officials and experts, who argue that the two cases have distinct characteristics. However, the possibility of a connection between the two killers remains a topic of fascination among conspiracy theorists and those who are looking for a broader pattern in unsolved American serial killings.

## 5. The "Psychiatric" Theory: A Killer with Psychological Motivations

The theory that Elizabeth Short's killer may have been driven by psychological issues has long been considered one of the more plausible explanations for her murder. Experts have frequently speculated that the brutality of the crime points to a killer with deep psychological problems, possibly someone with a history of mental illness or a warped sense of reality.

Elizabeth Short's murder, with its extreme violence and the dissection of her body, suggests a mind motivated by both sexual and sadistic impulses. Some experts have suggested that the killer may have had an unhealthy fixation on women, particularly women who fit a certain idealized or distorted image. Elizabeth Short, a young woman with Hollywood aspirations, could have been seen as embodying an ideal that the killer wanted to destroy or control. The display of her body in a public space, along with the detailed and methodical dissection, suggests a profound level of emotional detachment from the victim, which is often associated with individuals suffering from psychopathy or narcissistic personality disorders.

The profile of the Black Dahlia killer, according to those who support this theory, may resemble that of other known serial killers with psychological disorders. The careful and deliberate nature of the murder, the apparent lack of remorse, and the gruesome dismemberment suggest that the killer could have been someone with a deep sense of entitlement or a need for power and control. Many have argued that the killer's decision to pose Elizabeth Short's body in such a public and shocking manner was a reflection of a need for validation, recognition, and an exhibition of power. The psychological theory implies that the killer was motivated not just by sexual desires, but by a desire to dominate, manipulate, and intimidate society.

As with many of the theories surrounding the Black Dahlia case, the psychiatric theory is speculative, and its plausibility remains open to debate. However, it highlights the darker, more sinister nature of the crime and offers an explanation for the brutality and psychological complexity of the murder.

## 6. The "Professional" Theory: A Killer with Criminal Experience

A final theory to consider is that Elizabeth Short's murderer was a professional — someone with prior experience in violence, crime, or even medical procedures. This theory suggests that the killer had the knowledge and skill to dismember a body with precision and might have had prior experience either in law enforcement, the military, or another field that required a familiarity with violent tactics. The surgical nature of the dissection suggests someone with anatomical knowledge, and some believe that the killer might have been a doctor, a surgeon, or even someone with medical training.

In this theory, Elizabeth Short's death was the result of a calculated and deliberate act, and the killer may have chosen to engage in this horrific crime not out of impulse, but as a way to fulfill a deeper, darker psychological need. The careful disposal of the body — left in a vacant lot and positioned in a specific manner — suggests that the murderer was likely someone who had planned the crime in advance and understood how to cover their tracks. Additionally, this theory posits that the killer might have had prior knowledge of the area where the body was found, further supporting the idea of a person familiar with the city's geography and crime scene tactics.

While there is no concrete evidence to link any specific individual to the crime, this theory remains a compelling possibility. The exact nature of the crime — its methodical execution, the careful planning, and the precise handling of the body — points to someone with considerable criminal experience and a deep understanding of the act of murder.

# Part IV: Cultural Impact

# Chapter 9

## The Black Dahlia in Pop Culture

The Black Dahlia murder has become one of the most iconic unsolved crimes in American history, not only because of its gruesome nature but also because of the widespread cultural impact it had in the years following the discovery of Elizabeth Short's body. From the moment the case hit the front pages the case hit the front pages of newspapers in 1947, the Black Dahlia murder became a subject of fascination for the public. The horrifying details of Elizabeth Short's mutilation, combined with the sheer mystery surrounding her death, captured the imagination of the media and the public. Soon, the story was no longer just about a murder; it became an enduring symbol of the dark side of fame, Hollywood, and the seedy underbelly of Los Angeles. Over the years, the Black Dahlia would evolve from a tragic, real-life event into a cultural touchstone that continues to inspire countless portrayals in films, literature, and television.

The term "Black Dahlia" itself became synonymous with the murder, instantly evoking images of a tragic, beautiful woman whose life and death remain clouded in mystery. The media sensationalized Elizabeth Short's death, with some outlets romanticizing her image as a starlet on the verge of greatness, others painting her as a tragic victim of a malevolent world. This duality would come to define the portrayal of Elizabeth Short in popular culture. She would be mythologized as both an innocent, alluring beauty and a cautionary tale of the dark side of ambition.

In the years following the discovery of her body, the case permeated American culture, influencing filmmakers, novelists, and artists who saw in it the perfect blend of mystery, scandal, and the allure of Hollywood. The murder became not just a tragic event but a potent symbol of the American obsession with fame and beauty, and the often-brutal cost of that desire.

## Film, Literature, and Television

The Black Dahlia's cultural significance can be seen in the numerous films, books, and television series inspired by the case. Perhaps the most famous fictionalized account of the case came in 1987, when crime novelist James Ellroy published his noir crime novel *The Black Dahlia*. Ellroy's novel, which was later adapted into a 2006 film directed by Brian De Palma, blended historical facts with fiction, creating a world in which the unsolved murder became the backdrop for a story about obsession, corruption, and moral decay. While Ellroy's portrayal of the Black Dahlia murder deviated significantly from the real events, it captured the sense of mystery and dark allure that the case had taken on in the public imagination.

Ellroy's *The Black Dahlia* became a bestseller, and its success spawned a renewed interest in the case, particularly in how Hollywood had shaped its public perception. His novel also contributed to the theory that the case was part of a larger conspiracy involving the Los Angeles police force, organized crime, and the entertainment industry itself—a theory that would find echoes in later films and documentaries.

The Black Dahlia story has also appeared in other works of fiction. In the 1970s, crime author Raymond Chandler referenced the case in his novel *The Long Goodbye*. Chandler's depiction of Los Angeles in the mid-20th century was known for its gritty realism and moral ambiguity, both of which found a natural counterpart in the Black Dahlia case. Short's murder, Chandler suggested, was emblematic of the moral decay that ran through the city, corrupting even those who sought only to survive within its glitzy, star-studded veneer.

In addition to novels, the Black Dahlia murder has appeared in numerous films and television series, both as a focal point for plots and as a motif within larger narratives. TV shows like *American Horror Story* and *Castle* have included nods to Elizabeth Short's murder, often placing fictional characters into the real-life context of the investigation. The fact that her story continues to inspire pop culture adaptations speaks to the enduring nature of the mystery and the public's continued fascination with her tragic death.

# Fictionalized Accounts vs. Reality

One of the most striking aspects of the Black Dahlia case is the way in which reality and fiction have become so intertwined. Over the years, various theories, rumors, and sensationalized accounts have clouded the true story of Elizabeth Short's life and death, making it difficult for people to distinguish between the real and the imagined. This fusion of fact and fiction is part of what has fueled the cultural legacy of the case.

In the realm of fiction, many writers and filmmakers have taken creative liberties with the facts surrounding Short's life and murder. For example, in James Ellroy's *The Black Dahlia*, the focus is on two fictional detectives, Bucky Bleichert and Lee Blanchard, who become obsessed with solving the murder. Their obsession ultimately leads them to personal ruin, mirroring the sense of disillusionment that often characterizes the noir genre. However, the novel distorts key details about Elizabeth Short's life, her relationships, and her murder in order to explore themes of obsession and corruption. This departure from the true facts adds to the enduring mystery of the case, but it also makes it harder to separate the myth from the reality.

The 2006 film adaptation of *The Black Dahlia*, directed by Brian De Palma, also leaned heavily into the fictionalized narrative, with the investigation surrounding Elizabeth Short's death framed within a larger tale of police corruption, betrayal, and violence.

While the film borrowed the broad outline of the real events, it created an entirely new storyline with invented characters and speculative motivations for the crime. The result was a highly stylized, suspenseful thriller, but one that did little to clarify the truth behind Short's murder.

Similarly, in the world of true crime writing, many books have contributed to the mythmaking surrounding the Black Dahlia case. Some authors have speculated wildly about the identity of the murderer, pointing to high-profile figures like wealthy businessman George Hodel, while others have cast doubt on the legitimacy of the LAPD's investigation. These speculative accounts often blur the line between what is fact and what is conjecture, adding layers of intrigue and ambiguity that have made it impossible to reach any definitive conclusions about the case.

As the years have passed, the Black Dahlia murder has become more of a myth than a historical event. The fictionalized versions of Elizabeth Short's life and death are often more vivid and more widely circulated than the facts themselves. In this way, the murder has transformed into a cultural myth—a story that has evolved over time, shaped by the people who tell it.

## The Case as a Source of Inspiration

The Black Dahlia's cultural impact extends beyond its direct representations in film and literature; the case has also become a source of inspiration for other forms of art. Throughout the years, artists, musicians, and even fashion designers have drawn on the imagery of Elizabeth Short's life and murder, using her story as a lens through which to explore themes of beauty, violence, and the dark side of fame.

The most obvious example of this is the numerous works of visual art that have been inspired by the Black Dahlia case. Short's face, with her striking, wide-eyed gaze and haunting beauty, has been immortalized in paintings, photographs, and drawings. Many of these artworks focus on the stark contrast between her image as an aspiring actress and the brutal circumstances of her death, creating an eerie tension between the promise of Hollywood and the horror of her fate.

In music, the Black Dahlia has also found a place in the creative imagination. Several rock bands, particularly within the goth and alternative scenes, have written songs about Elizabeth Short, using her as a symbol of tragic beauty. These songs often focus on themes of obsession, decay, and the darker aspects of fame, much like the books and films that have centered on the case. The continued resonance of Elizabeth Short's story in contemporary music reflects the way in which her image has come to embody broader cultural anxieties about identity, desire, and the pursuit of fame.

Fashion designers, too, have been inspired by the Black Dahlia. The haunting imagery of Elizabeth Short, often depicted in black and white, has been used to sell everything from clothing to accessories. In some cases, designers have used her image as a symbol of glamour and tragedy, creating collections that evoke the glamour of 1940s Hollywood while also confronting the darker aspects of the starlet's life and death.

The Black Dahlia murder's long-lasting influence on popular culture is a testament to its enduring mystery and the way it taps into deeper cultural fears and fantasies. The case is not just about a woman's tragic death—it is a story that explores the dangerous allure of fame, the fragility of identity, and the blurred line between myth and reality. Over the decades, Elizabeth Short's name has become synonymous with Hollywood's darker side, and her story has inspired generations of artists, writers, and filmmakers to explore the complex interplay between beauty, fame, and violence. As long as her case remains unsolved, the Black Dahlia will continue to capture the imagination, fueling new generations of mystery-seekers and artists.

# Chapter 10

## Legacy of the Black Dahlia

### *The Influence on Popular Culture*

The Black Dahlia case has cast a long shadow over popular culture, leaving an indelible mark in the world of true crime, film, television, and literature. From the moment Elizabeth Short's mutilated body was discovered, the grisly nature of her murder captured the collective imagination of the public. The mystery of who killed her, the details surrounding her life, and the unanswered questions of why her death became a media sensation have fueled countless works of fiction and non-fiction.

Hollywood, with its deep connection to glamour and tragedy, was the perfect backdrop for the Black Dahlia story to become a cultural icon. The tale of a young woman with dreams of fame, whose life ended in a brutal and mysterious way, seemed to embody the darker side of the American dream. The glamour of Old Hollywood, the seduction of stardom, and the terror of a city filled with both possibility and danger all coalesced into a story that has fascinated people for decades.

Perhaps the most famous of these fictional portrayals is James Ellroy's 1987 novel *The Black Dahlia*, which reimagines the events surrounding Elizabeth Short's death through the lens of a fictionalized detective, Bucky Bleichert. The novel, and its subsequent film adaptation in 2006, not only retold the story of the murder but also dug into the corruption and decay of post-war Los Angeles. The Black Dahlia became a symbol of the city's fractured idealism, where dreams were pursued but often destroyed.

Ellroy's novel was notable not only for its vivid portrayal of the crime but also for its exploration of obsession, masculinity, and the darker facets of Los Angeles during the 1940s. The brutal depiction of Short's murder in the book and its psychological implications cemented her place in popular culture as a symbol of tragic beauty and unresolved mystery.

Outside of literature and film, the Black Dahlia case has been the subject of numerous documentaries and television shows. Its enigmatic nature lends itself well to true crime documentaries, where theories abound and experts dissect every possible clue. The public's fascination with the case has not waned over the decades, and new theories, discoveries, and suspects continue to surface, keeping the story alive.

Television shows like *American Horror Story: Hotel* (2015) have also incorporated elements of the Black Dahlia mythos, intertwining the true-life tragedy with fictional horror. In this case, the show uses the Black

Dahlia as a central theme in its narrative, referencing Elizabeth Short's murder as part of a larger tapestry of mysterious deaths and urban legends.

Additionally, many television crime dramas, such as *Cold Case*, have used the Black Dahlia as a touchstone, with episodes loosely inspired by the murder, emphasizing the cultural significance of the case even decades later. These adaptations and references demonstrate how Short's death has transcended its original context, becoming a permanent fixture in the world of popular culture, where it continues to be reinterpreted, sensationalized, and mythologized.

## *The Enduring Fascination with True Crime*

The Black Dahlia murder also played a crucial role in shaping the modern true crime genre. In the years following Short's death, the case became emblematic of the growing public interest in sensationalized criminal cases, particularly those that remained unsolved. The mystery surrounding Elizabeth Short's brutal murder fueled the rise of true crime stories in both journalistic and literary forms. As the case grew colder and the potential answers became more elusive, public fascination only intensified.

The gruesome nature of the crime, coupled with the media's relentless coverage, contributed to a society-wide obsession with violent crime and criminal psychology that continues to thrive today. Elizabeth Short's death was not just a tragic event; it became a cultural artifact, a dark mirror reflecting the anxieties of post-war America. The Black Dahlia case was one of the first true crime cases to receive such widespread media attention, and its impact can still be felt in the genre today.

The rise of the true crime genre in the latter half of the 20th century was bolstered by the Black Dahlia case. Stories like the Zodiac Killer, the Manson Family murders, and the Unabomber all followed in its wake, feeding the public's desire for suspenseful, often grisly narratives. The Black Dahlia case also contributed to a growing interest in criminal investigations, forensic science, and psychological profiling, fields that have since become central to both true crime storytelling and criminal investigations.

This cultural fascination shows no signs of waning. In the age of podcasts, documentaries, and streaming services, the Black Dahlia case continues to receive new attention. Shows like *The Case of the Black Dahlia* and *Unsolved Mysteries* have kept the story alive, presenting new theories and even reexamining old evidence. Elizabeth Short's murder remains one of the most enduring and unsettling unsolved crimes in American history, and the continued exploration of the case in popular media helps to maintain the mystery and allure that surrounds it.

## The Creation of a Myth

As the years have passed, the Black Dahlia has taken on a life of its own in American mythology. The combination of the gruesome murder and Elizabeth Short's tragic backstory has made her a symbol of both victimhood and mystery, a figure who lives on in the collective imagination. The idea of the "Black Dahlia" has evolved into more than just a nickname for Elizabeth Short—it has become a symbol of the dark side of Hollywood, the elusive nature of fame, and the frightening possibilities of a world where not everything is as it seems.

The "Black Dahlia" moniker itself has grown to represent not just the woman but the crime itself, evoking a sense of haunting elegance and horrific violence. In many ways, Elizabeth Short's image as the Black Dahlia embodies the duality of fame in Hollywood—the desire for recognition and success, but also the very real dangers of living in the public eye. Her story is often told through this lens, and the tragic irony that she was never truly famous, despite her death becoming the subject of widespread media attention, adds another layer of poignancy to her legacy.

The Black Dahlia is no longer just a cold case or a tragic story—she has become a part of American folklore. Her name is spoken in the same breath as other great unsolved mysteries, and her image—beautiful, enigmatic, and tragic—has become a staple in the history of American crime. She is a figure who stands for more than just her murder; she represents the allure and danger of fame, the dark underbelly of Los Angeles, and the haunting nature of unsolved mysteries that continue to captivate the public imagination.

The legacy of Elizabeth Short, the Black Dahlia, will likely endure for years to come. Her story continues to spark questions about the true nature of her death, the identity of her killer, and the cultural fascination that the case still evokes. Whether through documentaries, books, films, or conspiracy theories, the Black Dahlia remains an enduring and powerful symbol, forever etched in the annals of true crime history and American cultural memory.

# Part V: Theories, Speculations, and Unsolved Mysteries

# Chapter 11

# Theories and Speculations

Theories about the identity of Elizabeth Short's killer have ranged from the plausible to the absurd. Since the crime was never solved, the number of competing theories continues to grow, with new suspects and scenarios being introduced even in the present day. Below, we explore some of the most notable and widely discussed theories.

## 1. The Involvement of Multiple Killers

One of the most persistent theories is that Elizabeth Short's murder was not the work of a single individual but was instead the result of a group of people working in tandem. This idea stems from the brutality and meticulousness of the crime, with investigators and criminologists speculating that the precision with which Short's body was mutilated—particularly the clean, surgical-style cuts—could not have been the work of just one person. The theory suggests that there could have been multiple individuals involved in both the abduction and the execution of the murder, each playing a specific role in carrying out the crime.

This theory is not without merit. Some experts point to the fact that Short's body was found in a public park, indicating that the killer (or killers) may have planned to stage the scene for maximum shock value and public interest. Furthermore, the way in which Short's body was dissected—with clean incisions and the separation of certain body parts—led some to believe that the killer was either highly skilled or had help from others who were more familiar with anatomy or surgery.

## 2. The Black Dahlia as a Serial Killer's Signature Crime

Another prevailing theory is that the Black Dahlia murder was part of a broader pattern of serial killings. This theory suggests that Elizabeth Short's murder might have been committed by a serial killer who had previously—or would later—commit similar crimes in the same area. Proponents of this theory point to other unsolved homicides from the same period that bear similar characteristics, such as the use of precise dissection, the mutilation of the victim, and the positioning of the body.

Serial killer enthusiasts often highlight the parallels between the Black Dahlia case and the murders of women in the Los Angeles area during the 1940s and 1950s, suggesting that Short's murder was a part of a larger, undetected killing spree. The most notable example often cited is the murder of Jeanne French in 1946, whose body was similarly found in a public area, with signs of mutilation and sexual assault. While there is no definitive evidence linking these killings together, the similarities in the manner of death fuel the theory that Elizabeth Short's murderer may have been a serial killer who went on to commit other similar crimes in the following years.

## 3. The Role of the Hollywood Elite

One of the most sensational theories surrounding the Black Dahlia case suggests that Elizabeth Short's murder was not just a random act of violence but may have been the result of a sordid affair or conflict involving Hollywood elites. According to this theory, Short—whose dreams of becoming a movie star were well-known—was murdered due to her entanglement with powerful figures in the entertainment industry.

Supporters of this theory point to Elizabeth Short's connections to Hollywood parties, her reported relationships with wealthy men, and the suggestion that she was attempting to leverage those relationships to further her acting career. Some believe that she may have crossed paths with someone in the Hollywood elite who had something to lose if their connection with her were revealed. This theory is compounded by the notion that the murder was staged in such a way to send a message to others who might also be caught in compromising situations.

The idea that a member of Hollywood's elite could have been involved in such a gruesome crime was given some weight by individuals such as crime writer James Ellroy, whose novel *The Black Dahlia* explores this angle in fictionalized form. However, while there are many rumors and speculative accounts of Short's involvement with prominent men, there is little hard evidence to substantiate the claim that a Hollywood insider was directly responsible for her death.

## 4. The Los Angeles Police Department's Role

Some conspiracy theorists have raised the possibility that the Los Angeles Police Department (LAPD) itself may have been complicit in either the cover-up or mishandling of the investigation into Elizabeth Short's murder. Given the department's notorious history of corruption and inefficiency during the 1940s and 1950s, many argue that the LAPD could have failed to adequately pursue leads, destroy evidence, or even ignore crucial information that could have identified the killer.

The theory that the LAPD mishandled the investigation is supported by the numerous procedural missteps made during the early stages of the case. For example, there were reports that valuable evidence, such as photographs and witness statements, were either lost or disregarded. Some believe that the police may have been more focused on solving other high-profile cases, such as those involving gangsters or political figures, and simply let the Black Dahlia case fall into obscurity.

Others suggest that the department's incompetence in solving the case was rooted in a more systemic problem: a lack of interest in solving crimes involving women, especially women who were not wealthy or famous. In short, Short's status as a relatively unknown woman from out of town may have meant she wasn't viewed as a priority by the police, which allowed the investigation to stagnate.

## 5. The Connection to Other High-Profile Murder Cases

Another theory posits that Elizabeth Short's murder was connected to a broader web of high-profile murders and unsolved crimes in Los Angeles during the 1940s. This theory builds on the idea that Short's killing was not an isolated event but rather part of a larger pattern of crimes committed by a serial killer or organized group. Proponents of this theory point to the unsolved murders of other women during this period, such as the murders of Jeanne French and others who were killed in similar ways.

The most notable connection often discussed is the possibility that the Black Dahlia murder was linked to the infamous Zodiac Killer, a notorious serial killer who operated in Northern California during the late 1960s and early 1970s. Although the Zodiac Killer's crimes took place over a decade after Elizabeth Short's murder, some speculate that the Black Dahlia case was the killer's "first" high-profile murder, with the Zodiac continuing his spree of violence in the years that followed. While there is no hard evidence to support this claim, the similarities between the two killers' methods have made the connection a point of discussion for many amateur sleuths.

# Could the Black Dahlia Case Ever Be Solved?

### The Mystery of the Black Dahlia

The murder of Elizabeth Short, better known as the "Black Dahlia," remains one of the most infamous unsolved crimes in American history. The case continues to captivate the public, fueling speculation, theories, and countless investigative efforts. Despite the passage of time, the question of whether the crime could ever be solved lingers in the minds of true crime enthusiasts, historians, and investigators alike. In this section, we will explore various aspects of the case that suggest it may still hold the key to answers, as well as the reasons why it may remain unsolved.

# New Evidence and Advances in Technology

While the investigation into the Black Dahlia case has been marked by its many dead ends, there have been occasional breakthroughs and advances that offer new hope for solving the crime. One of the most significant developments in recent years has been the use of DNA analysis to re-examine old cases. Forensic DNA technology has revolutionized criminal investigations, offering the potential to revisit evidence from decades ago.

In 2003, the Los Angeles Police Department (LAPD) announced they had obtained new DNA evidence in connection to the case. Forensic experts analyzed the original evidence—most notably, a pair of stockings that had been found near Elizabeth Short's body. The hope was that a DNA profile could be extracted from the clothing and potentially linked to a suspect. However, the results were inconclusive, and it was revealed that the evidence contained both DNA from multiple sources and a mix of male and female genetic material. Despite this setback, some argue that the continued use of DNA analysis on the remaining evidence could eventually yield useful results. The significant advances in forensic science, particularly with genetic profiling and familial DNA searches, have given investigators new tools to uncover possible connections to the killer's descendants or even distant relatives who might be traced back through databases like Ancestry.com or 23andMe.

Despite these advances, the passage of time and the degradation of key physical evidence present substantial hurdles. The forensic evidence from 1947 was not preserved with the same protocols that are in place today, meaning that many critical pieces of evidence have deteriorated or been lost to history. Furthermore, the LAPD's reluctance to release certain files to the public has only fueled further speculation, with many believing that valuable evidence might still be locked away in police archives, preventing new leads from emerging.

# The Persistence of Eyewitness Accounts

Although many witnesses and people close to the case have come and gone over the years, several key eyewitness accounts still stand as points of interest in the ongoing investigation. Among the most famous claims are those of people who reported seeing Elizabeth Short with a mysterious man just days before her murder. Some of these accounts describe a tall, dark-haired man seen in the vicinity of Short's last known location, and others claim to have seen her with a man shortly before her final appearance in public.

Moreover, there were rumors in the early stages of the investigation that Elizabeth Short had been involved in a relationship with someone connected to the Hollywood elite—an affair that could have led to her murder. Several individuals who were either close to her or lived near her reported seeing strange behavior around the time of the crime. These types of eyewitness testimonies continue to be reevaluated, especially as new information and research come to light. Still, the lack of clear, corroborating evidence means that many of these accounts remain more speculative than definitive.

While eyewitness testimony could potentially serve as the catalyst for a breakthrough in the investigation, the passing of time has made it difficult for many of the people who were closest to the case to provide reliable or relevant details. A major obstacle in the resolution of the case lies in the unreliability of memory, especially given the sensationalistic nature of the crime and the media's involvement in sensationalizing every detail.

## Theories and Speculations: What Could Have Happened?

The question of whether the Black Dahlia case could ever be solved often brings the debate back to the many theories surrounding the identity of the killer and the events leading up to Elizabeth Short's murder. Over the decades, several high-profile suspects have emerged, each of whom has brought their own theory to the forefront. Some of the most notable and persistent theories include the idea that the murder was connected to organized crime, a Hollywood figure, or even a deranged lone killer with a personal vendetta against Short.

One of the most popular theories is the connection between Elizabeth Short and the Los Angeles underworld. Many theorists suggest that Short's brief stay in Hollywood and her lifestyle put her in the orbit of individuals with ties to organized crime. During the 1940s, Hollywood was rife with corruption, and the film industry was often intertwined with criminal activities. Some have speculated that Short may have crossed paths with a dangerous criminal figure who ultimately decided to silence her, either because of a personal vendetta or because she was perceived as a threat to a larger, more powerful network.

Another significant theory revolves around the idea that the killer was a figure in the Hollywood elite. According to some reports, Short had been seen with several men in the days leading up to her death, some of whom were in the entertainment industry. It has been suggested that she may have been the victim of a wealthy, influential person who had a motive for murder—whether because of a failed romantic relationship, jealousy, or an attempt to hide a scandalous affair.

Furthermore, there are those who believe the Black Dahlia murder could have been the work of a serial killer. The brutality of the crime and the meticulous way in which the body was disposed of bears similarities to other unsolved murders in the Los Angeles area during the same period. Some experts have drawn parallels to the so-called "Zodiac Killer," who terrorized California during the late 1960s, although no direct connection has ever been proven. Given the particularly gruesome nature of Short's death—her body was mutilated and drained of blood—the possibility of a serial killer or a highly skilled psychopath cannot be entirely dismissed.

Despite the wealth of theories, none of them have been conclusively proven, and many of the leads have since gone cold. Investigators have periodically revisited old suspects, but no new evidence has definitively linked anyone to the crime. The lack of a clear motive, combined with the incomplete nature of the investigation, means that even the most compelling theories remain speculative.

## Could New Witnesses Emerge?

In any cold case, the potential for new witnesses to emerge is always a hope for investigators. In the case of the Black Dahlia, there has been a continual flow of supposed confessions and tips from people who claim to have knowledge about the crime or the identity of the killer. Some of these individuals have even asserted that they knew Elizabeth Short personally or were in close proximity to her during her final days. While many of these claims have been dismissed as unreliable, some continue to add fuel to the fire.

For instance, in recent years, a woman who claims to be Elizabeth Short's half-sister came forward with new information that may shed light on the case. While her claims have not been verified, they add a new layer to the mystery of the Black Dahlia. Some people speculate that the key to solving the case may lie with descendants of those close to the victim—people who may have inherited pieces of the puzzle without fully understanding their significance.

Moreover, the digital age has made it easier for old witnesses and even distant relatives of individuals involved in the case to come forward. Social media platforms and forums dedicated to true crime have created spaces for people to share stories, even if they don't necessarily have definitive proof. It's possible that new information will surface through these platforms, and technology can facilitate the connection of dots that may have been missed in previous investigations.

## Why Is the Case So Difficult to Solve?

There are several factors that make the Black Dahlia case exceptionally difficult to solve. One of the primary reasons is the lack of physical evidence that could directly identify the killer. The crime scene was far from pristine—Elizabeth Short's body was discovered in a vacant lot, showing signs of significant trauma, but no witnesses came forward to report suspicious activity in the area. Additionally, there were no fingerprints on the body, and no DNA evidence tied to a specific individual.

Another complicating factor is the sensationalist media coverage that followed the discovery of Elizabeth Short's body. The case became a media circus, with newspapers publishing grotesque details about the crime and sensationalizing every aspect of Short's life. The media's portrayal of her as a "fallen woman" or "Hollywood hopeful" only added to the myth and mystique surrounding the case. In some cases, this led to the circulation of false leads, misinformation, and hoaxes that confused investigators. The sheer volume of tips, many of which were unfounded, made it difficult for authorities to discern the truth from the fiction.

Furthermore, the LAPD's investigation was reportedly hampered by internal issues. During the late 1940s, the department was dealing with corruption scandals and was not as equipped or efficient as it might have been in handling high-profile cases like the Black Dahlia murder. With multiple detectives and agencies involved, coordination was often poor, and key leads were sometimes overlooked or mishandled. As a result, the case became increasingly difficult to crack.

**The Case's Enduring Mystery**

The Black Dahlia case remains a haunting enigma, one that has sparked countless theories, investigations, and attempts at resolution. Despite the advances in forensic science and ongoing public interest in the case, the mystery of Elizabeth Short's brutal murder remains unsolved.

Whether the case can ever be solved depends on various factors: the discovery of new evidence, the potential for fresh witness testimony, and the ability of law enforcement to reexamine the case with new technological tools at their disposal. While the passage of time has certainly complicated the investigation, it has not entirely ruled out the possibility of a breakthrough.

Ultimately, the Black Dahlia case remains one of the most compelling and mysterious unsolved murders in American history. Despite the extensive investigations, theories, and countless books and films about the crime, Elizabeth Short's brutal death continues to puzzle both the public and law enforcement. In this section, we will explore whether there are any realistic paths forward in solving the case, the challenges involved, and the ongoing efforts to bring justice to Elizabeth Short.

**1. Advances in Forensic Technology**

One of the most important factors in determining whether the Black Dahlia case could ever be solved is the advancement of forensic technology. When Elizabeth Short's body was discovered in 1947, forensic science was not as advanced as it is today. The autopsy and investigation were limited by the techniques available at the time. For example, DNA testing was not yet a part of the investigative toolkit, and ballistics analysis was still in its infancy.

In the years since the crime, forensic science has evolved in significant ways, particularly in the areas of DNA analysis and genetic genealogy. DNA evidence, if present on the crime scene or on Short's body, could be instrumental in identifying a suspect or ruling out individuals who had been previously considered persons of interest. As technology improves, law enforcement agencies have begun to revisit cold cases with new methods, using everything from familial DNA to phenotyping to try to find answers.

The advent of genetic genealogy, which was famously used to identify the Golden State Killer in 2018, has the potential to revolutionize investigations into unsolved crimes like the Black Dahlia murder. By comparing DNA collected from crime scenes to public genealogy databases, investigators could potentially identify distant relatives of the killer, which could provide the breakthrough needed to solve the case. However, this method would still face significant hurdles in the Black

Dahlia case, as the evidence from 1947 may not be sufficient or well-preserved for this kind of analysis.

## 2. Challenges in Reopening the Case

Despite the technological advances, reopening a case that is nearly 80 years old presents unique challenges. One of the main difficulties is the preservation of physical evidence. In the 1940s, procedures for preserving forensic evidence were not as standardized as they are today. This means that much of the original evidence may have been mishandled or lost over the years. Additionally, the crime scene itself was not well protected, and evidence may have been contaminated by law enforcement, media, or bystanders who descended upon the scene in the chaotic hours following the discovery of the body.

Another challenge in reopening the Black Dahlia case is the sheer volume of information and false leads that have accumulated over the years. The case has attracted a wide range of amateur sleuths, journalists, and conspiracy theorists, each of whom has their own pet theories and suspects. With so much information and misinformation to sift through, investigators would need to carefully separate fact from fiction before pursuing any new leads. Given the public's enduring fascination with the case, law enforcement may also be under pressure to resolve it, which could potentially lead to hasty conclusions or misplaced priorities.

The sheer number of potential suspects is also a problem. Over the years, more than 500 individuals have been interviewed in connection to the Black Dahlia case, and at least 50 of them have been considered serious suspects. Some of these individuals were identified through tips or circumstantial evidence, while others were pursued after coming to the attention of the police or the media. Because so many people have been investigated, narrowing down the suspect list is a monumental task, especially when new suspects continue to surface from time to time.

### 3. Reexamining Old Suspects

While DNA analysis and modern investigative techniques offer new hope in solving the case, many experts believe that the solution might still lie within the existing pool of suspects. Throughout the years, a number of individuals have been proposed as potential killers, with varying degrees of evidence supporting their involvement. Revisiting these old suspects, armed with modern forensic tools, may be key to cracking the case.

One of the most notable suspects is George Hodel, a Los Angeles doctor who was suspected by several law enforcement officers and investigators. Hodel's name has remained associated with the Black Dahlia case for decades, due in part to the work of former LAPD detective Steve Hodel, who has spent years investigating his father's possible connection to the murder. Steve Hodel, in his books and media appearances, has argued that his father, George Hodel, was the killer. George Hodel was a prominent doctor in Los Angeles, and his behavior was both eccentric and suspicious, particularly after the murder.

In the years following the crime, Hodel was investigated but never charged. His son's investigation brought renewed attention to George Hodel's involvement, and some modern forensic experts believe that there may be a connection between Hodel and the crime. However, without conclusive DNA evidence, Hodel's involvement remains speculative.

Another well-known suspect is Leslie Dillon, a bellboy with a criminal history who was questioned by police shortly after the murder. Dillon's connection to the case is controversial, as he was considered a suspect due to circumstantial evidence and a series of odd behaviors. Some have argued that Dillon was involved in the crime, but again, no solid evidence ever linked him to the murder.

Despite these theories, most of the primary suspects in the case were eventually cleared, leaving behind an aura of uncertainty. Whether any of the individuals on the list of suspects are actually responsible for the crime remains one of the case's greatest mysteries.

## 4. The Role of the Public and Media in the Investigation

One of the central challenges in solving the Black Dahlia case is the role played by the media and the public in shaping the investigation. From the moment Elizabeth Short's body was discovered, the media frenzy surrounding the case reached a fever pitch. Sensationalized headlines, constant coverage, and public speculation dominated the narrative, making it difficult for investigators to conduct a focused, thorough investigation.

The attention paid to the case by the media also led to a number of false leads and mistaken conclusions. As various theories gained traction in the press, law enforcement was sometimes forced to chase down leads that had little to no basis in fact. The public, too, contributed to the investigation by submitting tips and potential suspects, many of which were entirely unfounded. In some cases, these false leads distracted from more promising avenues of investigation.

Moreover, the case became a symbol of the dark side of Hollywood, which contributed to its status as a true crime legend. The sensationalism surrounding the crime and its association with the glamorous and tragic image of Elizabeth Short only deepened the mystery, making it even more difficult to approach the case with objectivity and professionalism.

## 5. The Enduring Public Fascination

Despite all the failed attempts at solving the case, public interest in the Black Dahlia murder shows no signs of waning. Decades after Elizabeth Short's death, the mystery surrounding her brutal killing continues to captivate people around the world. The case remains a popular subject for books, documentaries, movies, and podcasts, all of which feed into the ongoing speculation about the true identity of her killer.

The enduring fascination with the Black Dahlia is driven by a number of factors. First, the crime itself is so brutal and unsettling that it is difficult to forget. The way in which Elizabeth Short was killed and the macabre nature of the crime scene has continued to haunt the public imagination. Additionally, the fact that the case remains unsolved after so many years only adds to its intrigue.

But perhaps most importantly, the case speaks to larger societal fears and obsessions. The Black Dahlia murder has become a symbol of the dark underbelly of Hollywood, representing the tragic intersection of fame, ambition, and violence. Elizabeth Short, who dreamed of becoming a star, has become an icon of lost potential, and the mystery of her death represents a gap in our understanding of both the past and human nature itself.

## 6. Conclusion: Could the Case Be Solved?

The Black Dahlia case, while one of the most infamous unsolved murders in American history, may never be solved in a traditional sense. With so many years gone by and so much of the physical evidence lost or destroyed, it is unlikely that a simple answer will emerge. However, as advancements in forensic technology continue to evolve, there is still hope that new techniques could provide the breakthrough needed to close the case.

Ultimately, the Black Dahlia remains an enduring mystery—a crime that will likely never be fully explained. As time passes, however, there will always be those who continue to search for answers, driven by the need to understand the true story of Elizabeth Short and the circumstances of her tragic death.

# Epilogue

## *Reflection on Elizabeth Short's Life and Death*

### The Woman Behind the Mystery

In the years since her tragic death, Elizabeth Short has been transformed from a young woman with dreams of stardom into an enigmatic symbol of a cold, unsolved crime. Yet, beyond the media frenzy and public fascination, it is important to remember the person she was before she became a notorious figure in true crime history. Elizabeth Short was born on July 29, 1924, in Boston, Massachusetts, to Cleo and Phoebe Short. Her early life, though marked by hardship, was far from the gruesome narrative that would later consume her memory.

Her father abandoned the family when Elizabeth was just a child, and she grew up in a tumultuous environment, with a mother who struggled to support her. Elizabeth's path to Hollywood was not an immediate one. Like many young women during the 1940s, she moved westward with hopes of becoming an actress, though she lacked formal training and connections in the film industry. Her story mirrors that of many hopefuls who came to Los Angeles, their dreams of fame unfulfilled and their lives often shrouded in obscurity.

While much of what is known about Elizabeth's life is colored by sensationalist media coverage, there are glimpses of a young woman who longed for more. She was described as friendly and outgoing, someone who had a certain allure, but she was not without her own struggles. Accounts of her interactions with friends and family paint a picture of a woman who was sometimes introspective, conflicted about her future, and trapped in an ever-present tension between her ambitions and the harsh realities of life.

Her death, as violent and brutal as it was, should not overshadow the fact that Elizabeth Short was a person—a woman with her own aspirations, relationships, and challenges. In some ways, her murder has eclipsed the fullness of her life, and in seeking answers to the mystery of her death, it is essential to not lose sight of who she was before she became the Black Dahlia.

## A Lasting Legacy in the Crime and Media Landscape

The Black Dahlia case remains one of the most infamous unsolved murders in American history. Its legacy has shaped the landscape of true crime investigations and media coverage. It also raised profound questions about the relationship between crime, media, and public interest. The overwhelming fascination with Elizabeth Short's murder has led to an ever-expanding universe of theories, books, films, and documentaries, ensuring that her name will remain linked to mystery for generations to come.

Over the decades, the Black Dahlia case has become a symbol of both the allure and danger of fame. Elizabeth Short's desire for a Hollywood career and her tragic fate serve as a cautionary tale for many, a reminder of how dreams can go awry and how a single act of violence can reshape a person's life and legacy in ways that no one could predict.

The case has also been a vehicle for exploration into the darker aspects of human nature, from the psychology of the potential killer(s) to the ethics of media sensationalism. The public's relentless need for closure has been met with frustration, as authorities have failed to uncover definitive answers. This has resulted in numerous conspiracy theories, amateur investigations, and endless speculation. The case is emblematic of the larger societal fascination with unsolved mysteries and the darker aspects of human nature.

However, it also speaks to a certain collective yearning for justice. While the mystery surrounding Elizabeth's death may never be solved, the case has served to highlight issues within the Los Angeles Police Department's practices in the 1940s, the vulnerabilities of young women in a predatory environment like Hollywood, and the complex relationship between crime and celebrity.

## Reflection on the Search for Closure

The search for answers in the Black Dahlia case has never truly ended. Over the decades, the Los Angeles Police Department has revisited the case multiple times, most recently in the 2000s, with the hopes of identifying new evidence or employing modern forensic techniques. DNA analysis, for example, has offered some hope that breakthroughs may be on the horizon. However, despite advances in forensic technology and public interest in the case, no definitive conclusions have emerged.

This ongoing pursuit of justice reveals the persistence of the human desire for closure. The Black Dahlia case is more than just a crime; it represents a cultural obsession with unresolved mysteries and a longing for resolution in a world that often seems to withhold it. Elizabeth Short's brutal murder, and the lack of closure surrounding it, serves as a reminder that not all stories have a neat and tidy ending. The search for the truth continues to captivate public imagination, making the Black Dahlia case a touchstone in discussions of crime, justice, and the darker side of human behavior.

## Elizabeth Short's Enduring Mystique

While the Black Dahlia case remains unsolved, Elizabeth Short's legacy endures through the myths, theories, and cultural artifacts that have grown around her. Her image has become synonymous with mystery, the dark allure of Hollywood, and the brutality of an unresolved crime. Her story, tragic as it may be, has inspired countless artists, writers, filmmakers, and true crime enthusiasts.

There is something inherently tragic about Elizabeth Short's story—her life, her dreams, and her untimely death. And yet, it is the mystery of her murder that has elevated her into the realm of legend. It is through this lens that she is remembered, not as a simple woman who lived and died but as a symbol of something much larger—the dangers of fame, the darkness that can lurk in seemingly idyllic places, and the enduring power of mystery in human culture.

Her story, like so many other unresolved mysteries, refuses to fade into obscurity. Every new generation continues to uncover pieces of her narrative, adding to the ever-expanding mythology of the Black Dahlia. In a sense, Elizabeth Short has become a timeless figure, whose tragic end has kept her relevant in the annals of history.

## Moving Forward: A Call for Resolution

Though the passage of time has only deepened the complexity of the Black Dahlia case, there remains hope that one day the truth may come to light. Advances in technology, shifts in investigative practices, and an ongoing public interest may eventually provide the breakthrough needed to solve the case. For now, the mystery continues to live on, not as a simple account of a crime, but as a story that reflects the fragility of human life and the ongoing pursuit of justice.

In the end, Elizabeth Short's story is both one of tragedy and one of resilience. Though she may have entered the public consciousness as the victim of an unsolved crime, her life—and the questions surrounding her death— serve as a poignant reminder of the human desire for justice, closure, and a deeper understanding of the darker sides of our society.

Her name will continue to haunt the pages of history, a symbol of the endless quest for answers in a world where some questions may never be fully answered. The Black Dahlia remains a mystery that refuses to die, much like the woman whose life it was once part of—a life that, even in death, continues to captivate the imagination of the public.

# Appendices

## Timeline of the Case

**1947**

- **January 15**: Elizabeth Short, known posthumously as the Black Dahlia, is last seen alive at the Biltmore Hotel in downtown Los Angeles.
- **January 15–16**: Elizabeth Short's body is discovered in a vacant lot at 39th Street and Norton Avenue, approximately 10:00 AM. The body is severed at the waist, and the remains are posed grotesquely, with the mouth slashed into a gruesome smile and the body drained of blood. The body is found by a woman named Betty Bersinger, who initially believes the corpse to be a discarded mannequin.
- **January 17**: The Los Angeles Police Department (LAPD) officially begins its investigation. Detectives initially focus on finding Short's identity, and she is quickly linked to her photograph, which is published widely.
- **January 21**: Elizabeth Short's identity is confirmed through her fingerprints. The media picks up the story, and the press begins calling her the "Black Dahlia," referencing a popular film noir, *The Blue Dahlia*, which had been released

earlier that year. The name sticks, cementing her place in history.

- **February 14**: The Los Angeles Examiner receives a disturbing package containing Elizabeth Short's birth certificate, photographs, and other personal items. The sender claims to be the killer, though the authenticity of the letter is debated. The package is a major turning point in the case, confirming that the murderer is closely following the media coverage.
- **March 1947–January 1948**: Despite the barrage of tips from the public, no solid leads or suspects emerge. The investigation shifts towards focusing on Short's personal life, including her relationships with men, her residence in California, and her lifestyle in the city.
- **October 15, 1947**: A key suspect, Robert Manley, who had been involved with Elizabeth Short just before her death, is interviewed extensively but ultimately cleared of any involvement in her murder.
- **July 1, 1948**: The LAPD officially closes the case as a "cold case," though rumors and theories about the Black Dahlia murder continue to swirl for decades.

## List of Investigating Authorities

1. **Los Angeles Police Department (LAPD)**: The primary agency responsible for investigating the

Black Dahlia case. Detective Harry Hansen, along with other members of the LAPD's Homicide Division, were assigned to the case immediately after Short's body was discovered.

2. **Detective Harry Hansen**: One of the lead investigators, Hansen was a seasoned LAPD detective who worked the case from its early stages. He was deeply involved in questioning witnesses and following up on leads.

3. **Detective Paul F. Reilly**: Another key member of the LAPD's investigative team, Detective Reilly was one of the officers who spoke to Elizabeth Short's family and friends, piecing together more details about her life.

4. **Lieutenant Edward O'Donnell**: The head of the Homicide Division at the time, O'Donnell oversaw the Black Dahlia investigation in its early days and would later comment on the confusing and mysterious aspects of the case.

5. **Los Angeles Examiner**: While not directly involved in the investigation, the Los Angeles Examiner, under editor James Richardson, was instrumental in publicizing the case. The newspaper received several letters, including one allegedly from the killer, which became a central part of the case's intrigue.

6. **FBI**: The Federal Bureau of Investigation provided forensic and investigative support during the case but did not officially take charge. The agency would also take a more active role in the case in later years as new leads emerged.

7. **Coroner's Office**: The Los Angeles County Coroner's Office conducted the post-mortem examination of Elizabeth Short's body. Dr. Frederick Newbarr, the Chief Medical Examiner, was the one who first reported on the extreme nature of the mutilation.

## Suspects and Theories

Several names have been linked to the Black Dahlia case over the years, but no one has ever been definitively proven to be responsible for Elizabeth Short's death. Theories have ranged from involvement by well-known figures to more obscure suspects. Here is a brief list of some of the most discussed names in connection with the case:

1. **George Hodel**: A prominent Los Angeles doctor, Hodel is often considered a prime suspect in the Black Dahlia case. His name resurfaced in the 2000s following the release of evidence by his son, Steve Hodel, a former LAPD detective. George Hodel was reportedly close to some members of the Hollywood elite and had a history of violent behavior. In *Black Dahlia Avenger*, Steve Hodel argues that his father was the killer, citing circumstantial evidence and his father's known connections to Los Angeles crime scenes.

2. **Robert Manley**: A former boyfriend of Elizabeth Short, Manley was initially considered a prime suspect because he was one of the last people to

see Short alive. However, after multiple interrogations, Manley was cleared of any involvement, and no direct evidence linked him to the murder.

3. **Leslie Dillon**: A bellboy with a history of mental instability, Dillon was questioned by the LAPD in the 1950s. He had peculiar knowledge about the crime scene and had made strange statements about the case, though no charges were ever brought against him. Some theorists believe Dillon had connections to the murder, possibly as an accomplice, but evidence remains lacking.

4. **The "Man in the Black Suit"**: In the years following the crime, some witnesses came forward to claim they had seen a mysterious man near the crime scene or with Elizabeth Short in the days leading up to her death. These reports have remained inconclusive, and the identity of the so-called "man in the black suit" is unknown.

5. **The LAPD's Own Officers**: Some conspiracy theories suggest that members of the LAPD might have been involved in covering up the case. These theories are bolstered by allegations of corruption and misconduct within the police department in the 1940s. However, these claims have never been substantiated.

**Notable Publications and Books**

1. **"The Black Dahlia" by James Ellroy (1987)**: One of the most well-known fictionalizations of the case, Ellroy's novel *The Black Dahlia* imagines a detective's pursuit of a woman's killer in a Los Angeles steeped in corruption, excess, and deception. While a work of fiction, Ellroy's book has influenced the cultural memory of Elizabeth Short and her tragic fate.

2. **"Black Dahlia Avenger" by Steve Hodel (2003)**: This book explores the theory that Steve Hodel's father, Dr. George Hodel, was responsible for the Black Dahlia murder. Using a combination of police reports, personal accounts, and circumstantial evidence, Steve Hodel presents a compelling argument for his father's guilt, despite the lack of a formal conviction.

3. **"The Black Dahlia Files" by Don H. Wolfe (1996)**: A detailed investigation into the Black Dahlia case, Wolfe's book assembles a range of evidence, police reports, and interviews to present a narrative of the events surrounding Elizabeth Short's life and murder. The book also explores the various theories that have arisen over the decades regarding the identity of the killer.

4. **"The Black Dahlia Haunting" (2012)**: A speculative account of the case, this book weaves together fiction and theory to explore the possibility of supernatural forces at play in the mystery surrounding Short's death.

Made in the USA
Coppell, TX
18 January 2025

44598944R00075